Profit by Investing in STUDENT HOUSING

Cash In On the Campus Housing Shortage

Michael H. Zaransky

 PUBLISHING

President, Kaplan Publishing: Roy Lipner
Vice President and Publisher: Maureen McMahon
Acquisitions Editor: Victoria Smith
Senior Managing Editor: Jack Kiburz
Typesetter: the dotted i
Cover Designer: Scott Rattray, Rattray Design

Published by Kaplan Publishing,
a division of Kaplan, Inc.

Printed in the United States of America

06 07 08 10 9 8 7 6 5 4 3 2 1

Library of Congress Cataloging-in-Publication Data

Zaransky, Michael H.
Profit by investing in student housing : cash in on the campus housing shortage / Michael H. Zaransky.
     p.   cm.
Includes index.
ISBN-13: 978-1-4195-2188-1
ISBN-10: 1-4195-2188-8
   1. Real estate investment—United States. 2. Student housing—United States—Finance. I. Title.
   HD1382.5.Z37   2006
   332.63'243—dc22

                                                                    2005034239

DEDICATION

I dedicate this book to my wife and high school sweetheart, Barbara, and our two extraordinary children, Brad and Karen. You are all so much more than any man can ever hope for. You are my true wealth and passion. I love each of you so very much.

Writing and publishing this book has been an especially rewarding experience for me. I have a passion for real estate investing and receive a great deal of satisfaction from writing. Having the opportunity to blend two of the activities I enjoy so much—real estate and writing—is a tremendous opportunity for which I am most appreciative. Publishing a book has always been one item on my list of things I had hoped to accomplish "one day." This book allows me to check off that one item with a rewarding feeling and a source of personal satisfaction.

As I have matured, I've come to realize that life's most important things are the relationships we have with other people. I have been fortunate to have developed many special relationships that add meaning to my life and profoundly affect my success. Certainly the completion and publication of this book—the fulfillment of one of my goals—would not have been possible without the help and encouragement of many.

As I reflect on the path my personal and professional life has followed, I know that I've been fortunate and have many people to thank for it. My parents, Roz and Dave Zaransky, have always been there with unconditional support and love. Our parents would do everything and anything for their three sons. Indeed, they paid for and encouraged my entire (and expensive) education without complaining or seeking recognition. They've encouraged me and taken pride in all my successes. They've stood by me—equally committed—in my toughest times.

My in-laws, Jack and Lillian Mangurten, have always been among my biggest cheerleaders. Immigrants to this country after surviving the atrocities of the Holocaust, they started in the

United States with nothing and continue to serve as a source of awe. They act as role models for our entire family.

Entrepreneurship is infectious and often passed on to subsequent generations. My maternal grandfather, Meyer Katzman, whom I never knew because he died at a young age, was the first in my family to enter the real estate investment business. His example, mentoring, and entrepreneurial spirit influenced my father to enter the business. My father, in turn, influenced my decision to enter the family profession for a third generation. I owe a great deal of gratitude to my grandfather for passing on this great gift.

Outside the family, I've heard wonderful things about Grandfather Katzman and the fine reputation he earned in the real estate industry. Even though I never knew him, he continues to have a profound effect on me. I'd love to talk with him today. I hope he's proud of me.

My wife and ace proofreader, Barbara, has encouraged me in all of my personal and professional endeavors. No matter what bumps life threw our way, she never stopped giving me her confidence and encouragement. Without Barbara's constant support, I would have never completed or published this book. She kept telling me that I could and should write it!

My son, Brad, and daughter, Karen, were equally supportive and encouraging of this effort. My kids are a great source of pride to me. It's been one of my true joys in life to see them mature into young adults I feel proud of. To have their encouragement and pride for my own accomplishments is a great source of satisfaction.

My partner at Prime Property Investors, Ltd., Barbara Gaffen—a dear friend and business partner—is wonderful to be in business with. Together we make a great team. Each day is a creative collaboration between us. I love coming to the office and, although I enjoy my weekends, I always look forward to Monday. Although we never know where deals will come from or where real estate trends will take us, we do know that together we'll continue to accomplish great things. Barbara Gaffen has also been supportive of my book-publishing efforts; she's been especially helpful in letting me bounce ideas off her and offering worthwhile suggestions.

I want to acknowledge and thank the great people at Kaplan Publishing and especially Senior Acquisitions Editor Mary B. Good, who first approached me with the idea for this book. A true professional, she has been easy to work with throughout the publishing process. I thank my copy editor, Barbara McNichol, another true professional whose suggestions and edits made the finished product a book I feel proud of.

Over a number of years in the real estate business, I have met many real estate professionals and learned from almost every encounter and transaction with them. I credit my relationships with them as the major reason for my successes. As competitive as the real estate business may seem to those on the outside, I have found, with few exceptions, that most real estate professionals willingly assist others in the business. I have learned so much from so many too numerous to mention. I appreciate the opportunities so many have given me.

Consider this book my way of giving back to all—by sharing my knowledge and experience in the student housing niche.

Contents

THE LATEST, GREATEST INVESTMENT NICHE

I love real estate and the real estate investment business. I grew up with real estate in my blood. I am the third generation in my family to actively own and operate real estate investment property. Despite the entry of large firms, publicly traded real estate investment trusts (REITs), and institutional money investors, real estate is still the turf of individual entrepreneurs. I love that! Although I had a head start and was able to use family money to conduct my first real estate deals, I have many friends in the business who started with absolutely nothing. In fact, it's common in the real estate business to meet multimillionaire property owners who started with no money of their own and, through hard work, built a net worth in the millions of dollars.

Real estate entrepreneurs are fun and creative people. It is a blast going to work every day. I am so fortunate I can engage in my passion for making real estate deals and making money doing it. It's not work; I'm having too much fun!

At our company, we never know for certain when our next deal will come, but we do know it will be challenging and engaging. Make no mistake; there is no "cookie-cutter approach" to the real estate business.

Most successful real estate investors specialize in one or two property categories. Sure, some successful investors have investments in a variety of property types, but they are rare. At least, I don't know any—and, trust me, I know many people in the real estate investment business.

A number of property types, or asset classes, exist within the real estate investment community. The most common general property categories include industrial, retail, multifamily, and office. (Other specific property subclasses in which to invest include raw land, mobile homes, hotels, self-storage, parking garages, and entertainment.)

While similarities exist in all property types and real estate transactions, each asset class has its own set of issues and specific characteristics that make property-type real estate investor specialists most successful. For example, my partner and I have succeeded by specializing in the multifamily apartment building property asset class. We learn everything we can about apartment buildings. Every day, we contact property owners, real estate agents, and lending sources that specialize in the multifamily apartment building asset class.

Within this class, we have found success by even further specializing—always looking for more specific niche categories within the asset class. For instance, we've had success within this category in vintage apartment building renovation and repositioning, condominium conversions, and distressed property turnaround. In this fluid and ever-changing business, we're always on the lookout for a new or developing niche within our specialty.

I figure if we find an exciting real estate investment niche, learn everything about it, network with the most active leaders in the niche, and look at lots of potential transactions, no one will excel at it better than us! With so much in the world of investing that's uncertain and beyond one's control, I've learned to select higher yield investments in which favorable demographics drive continued demand for the property. In searching for a lucrative real estate investment niche, there is nothing better than finding a property asset class with a bright future—and one that's driven by demographic trends in the investors' favor.

Within the asset class of multifamily apartment buildings, I have found that niche—and I don't believe anyone knows more about it than my partner and me. It's the student housing apartment niche.

Indeed, I have read everything available, attended every conference possible, published articles on the subject, and belong to every quality trade association involved in the student housing business. As the co-CEO of a company active in the acquisition of student housing properties on major university campuses throughout the country, I feel confident knowing we have come close to mastering this market. We know every college campus that is a potential good market of opportunity. We know how to analyze a potential acquisition and make an offer that will get accepted. We know how to put the financing together to get a deal closed.

Over the years, I've learned the value of patience, research, and opportunity. We gather all the data we can about our selected niche, learn about our targeted markets of opportunity, and become a known acquirer within the business. Then, when the right deal becomes available, we pounce. We also know the potential pitfalls inherent in the student housing investment niche, so we're constantly taking measures to control the downside in any transaction. Perhaps most important, we have learned when to walk away from a student housing transaction that's overpriced or too risky.

This book shares the knowledge and insights I've gained as an active participant in the *next great thing* in real estate investing—the student housing real estate investment niche. May you learn from my mistakes and successes by reading this book!

WHY STUDENT HOUSING?

Unlike traditional residential investment real estate transactions, student housing property returns are influenced by a unique set of factors. Student housing properties in a particular college town achieve high occupancy levels when (1) enrollment at the university is high and (2) available alternative housing choices are in short supply. This may sound oversimplistic but, in a nutshell, that is all there is to it.

Student housing has a great future, and my company has jumped in with both feet (and more) because we are convinced that the future is bright. A coming student housing shortage on most major university campuses will drive up rents and cash flow for college town property owners and, as a result, supercharge property values and investor net worth. When you finish reading

Part One, you will see what I mean and want to get in the game as well!

Chapter 1 takes you through the irreversible demographic trends that will drive the demand for student housing into the next decade and beyond. Chapter 2 introduces you to my proven techniques for choosing a university campus that has the greatest potential for a successful student housing real estate investment.

1

DEMOGRAPHICS DRIVE DEMAND FOR STUDENT HOUSING

As the new school year begins each fall, cars, vans, trucks, and trailers are loaded with a semester's worth of personal belongings and school supplies. A pilgrimage hits the national highway system as millions of American young adults begin the new college school year. Once on campus, the unloading begins as freshmen move into the dormitory lounges or multipurpose rooms. For many, this is a "temporary" housing measure as they wait for a scarce dorm room bed to become available.

As if it isn't enough trauma for 18-year-olds to be away from home for the first time, each fall tens of thousands of students find themselves stuck in the purgatory of temporary housing arrangements. That's because many college campuses in the United States suffer from severe student housing shortages. For example:

- The University of Arkansas was forced to book students without dorm rooms into the local Holiday Inn Express at the beginning of a recent fall term. The university quickly scurried to rent private apartments in the college town to house 288 students who didn't have places to live.

- Because of student housing shortages at the University of California at Irvine, many students have taken up residence at nearby trailer parks.
- At Rutgers University, the waiting list for on-campus school-owned housing has been 1,000+ names long for the past several years.
- Many public colleges and universities are taking out master leases on entire apartment complexes near their campuses to house students closed out of crowded university-owned dorms.

Student housing trauma stories are becoming the rule, not the exception. Increasingly, most major public university campuses experience a shortfall in providing enough dorm rooms to house the influx of students. When it comes to housing students on college campuses around North America, something is definitely up—but what exactly is it?

WHY IT'S A HOT REAL ESTATE INVESTMENT OPPORTUNITY

For investors, "getting smart" means moving into the student housing real estate niche. Student housing provides higher rates of return with lower levels of risk than do traditional residential rental properties and are more likely to substantially appreciate in value. The need for privately owned near-campus student housing will be greatly enhanced because of three factors:

1. Members of the echo boom generation are reaching college age, boosting the number of people turning 18 to 80 million over the next decade.

2. An increasing percentage of high school graduates are enrolling in colleges and universities than ever before.
3. Public universities are under increasing financial pressure because of state budget deficits. This crisis limits the funds available to pay for additional university-owned student housing.

The Echo Boom Generation

Yes, the children of the baby boom generation are reaching college age. The sons and daughters of this large generation make up a population segment as numerous as that of their parents. You've probably seen this in the popular culture. With so many in this age group, the echo boomers have become the darlings of the retail and advertising world. Madison Avenue and music labels love to market and sell to this large group of teens.

Most significantly for real estate investors, echo boomers are going to college in record numbers, sustaining a postsecondary education enrollment boom for years to come. According to a 2004 study by the National Multi Housing Council (NMHC) titled "Student Housing 101: Where are the Opportunities?", student housing is becoming one of the apartment industry's most important niche opportunities as a result of the increasing number of college-age students.

These facts back up that conclusion:

- According to U.S. Census Bureau statistics, children of the baby boom generation born between 1977 and 1997 are 80 million strong. At its peak year in 1990, the bureau recorded 4.1 million births of echo boomers.
- The birthrate of echo boomers in 1990 represented an increase of 25 percent over the 1977 birthrate. Today, this group is seeking a postsecondary education.

- In 2003, four million Americans turned 18. The number of young people turning 18 will continue to increase over the next ten years when, in 2010, it will peak at 4.4 million. Thus, large numbers of the population reaching college age will continue and will remain above four million annually to 2020.

These compelling figures explain why millions of young people will be heading for university campuses in time for the fall semester. And they will require housing. Unlike predicting a fashion trend or the next movie hit, investors know with 100 percent certainty that millions of consumers will seek to rent student housing near university campuses for many years to come. As the demand for this housing increases, rents will rise. Therefore, smart investors who get into this market will likely see their cash flow and net worth skyrocket.

College Degrees Highly Desirable

What's more, not only is the population of potential student housing consumers increasing in size, but also the choice to pursue a college degree is increasing in popularity. In years gone by, obtaining a postsecondary school education was a plum résumé builder and an honor achieved by a select minority. Now, the majority of high school graduates enter college if they want to pursue white-collar or professional career opportunities. The Census Bureau indicates that in 2002, approximately 65 percent of high school graduates enrolled in a college or university—a significant increase from the 45 percent who entered postsecondary schools in 1997.

DREAM-COME-TRUE BUSINESS

Can there be a better dream-come-true business than providing housing for a guaranteed market well into the future? Today, the number of consumers eligible for the student housing product is growing; so is the percentage of market share for eligible consumers demanding housing. Compare this trend to a pharmaceutical company marketing a wonder drug that controls cholesterol for over-50s. This hypothetical drug is better than others available and has no side effects. In addition, its target age group keeps growing in size, *plus* 20 percent more people in this group are experiencing high cholesterol. Given the demographic trends in this fictional scenario, the likelihood of selling a huge volume of this cholesterol drug is high. As a smart investor, you'd want to purchase as much of this drug company's stock as you could afford!

No Stopping This Trend

In the student housing market, a similar demographic trend isn't fictional. There's no stopping this trend. As the echo boomers give birth to their own children, and as families continue to immigrate to the United States, the trend will continue and the student housing market will boom for decades to come.

Clearly, increases in college enrollment have already begun. See the chart in Figure 1.1, which was prepared from data provided by the U.S. Department of Education.

Approximately 16.4 million students were enrolled in postsecondary school institutions of higher learning during 2003. The 2003 enrollment figure represents an increase of 14.6 percent over the past ten years, adding two million students to the college and university enrollment figures. The U.S. Department of Education has projected that enrollments will remain strong, climbing to 18.2 million by 2013.

This echo boom spike in enrollments will be followed by the children of the echo boomers, called the millennial boom generation. As a result, during the next decade alone, the federal government projects an increase of 1.8 million in enrollments. What

FIGURE 1.1 *College Enrollment, 1988–2013 (in thousands)*

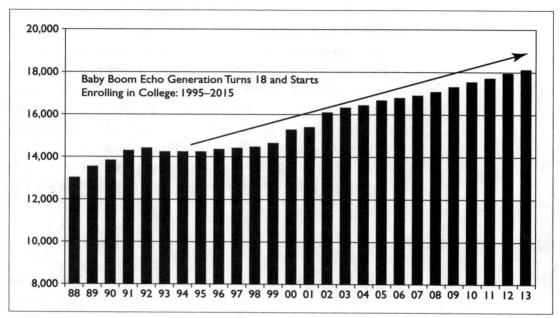

Baby Boom Echo Generation Turns 18 and Starts
Enrolling in College: 1995–2015

Source: U.S. Department of Education.

does that mean to investors? Future students (and renters) are alive and waiting in the wings.

EXISTING STUDENT HOUSING SHORTAGE

Of 127 colleges and universities recently surveyed by *College Planning and Management Magazine,* on-campus school-owned student housing served, on average, only 30.12 percent of the total current student population. Of the 73 public universities included in the survey, the on-campus school-owned bed capacity accommodated only 25.98 percent of the total students (according to "College Housing 2005 Special Report" in *College Planning and Management Magazine,* June 2005). The remaining and projected increasing number of students must look for housing off campus.

That means well-located private student housing apartment buildings will continue to achieve high occupancy levels and increased cash flow.

In the course of my active real estate investment career and ten-year service on the loan committee of a Chicago suburban bank, I have analyzed the numbers and reviewed financial statements for hundreds (perhaps thousands) of real estate investment properties. Studying statements and purchase prices for thousands of traditional and student housing investment properties has caused me to reach several compelling conclusions. It is not uncommon for well-located student housing buildings to achieve occupancy levels of 98 percent to 100 percent with little or no rent collection loss. Occupancy levels and the ratio of rental income to operating expenses are often far superior in the student housing niche compared with that of traditional apartment buildings. As an investor, you can experience a decent cap rate spread between traditional and student housing apartment transactions. They result in positive cash flow and above-average return on equity for well-financed and well-researched student housing deals.

Furthermore, university and college enrollments are tied to the size of the post-high-school population, not to external economic factors. As a result, the student housing market has remained immune to the vacancy problems experienced in the traditional multifamily sector, which is tied to job markets and employment rates.

BUDGET CONSTRAINTS LIMIT BUILDING UNIVERSITY-OWNED DORMS

At the same time as the number of students seeking a post-secondary-school education increases, university-owned dorms are aging and state-funded institutions of higher learning are falling under severe budgetary constraints. Indeed, the fiscal health of many states has worsened in recent years, forcing state governments to make substantial cuts across the board. Not surprising, allocations to public universities have not been immune to budget cutting; therefore, little, if any, public money is available to fund construction of on-campus dorms at major universities. Instead, limited funds go into improving academic programs rather than into housing.

To that add the fact that health care and primary education compete for funds. These categories have traditionally received budget priority over higher educational institutions from state legislatures. Because of budget pressures and the political realities of priorities, university finances are experiencing greater financial pressure than ever at a time when student enrollments and demand for postsecondary education are skyrocketing.

That's why most universities are cutting both operating and capital expenditure budgets. Tuition increases can't possibly keep pace. Colleges and universities just don't have the money required to build enough dorm rooms to meet student housing demands. This clearly indicates that universities will need to rely on the private sector to house the coming echo boomers as they enroll in college by the millions. This state budget crisis makes the student housing niche opportunity even more appealing!

THE DEMANDS OF TODAY'S STUDENTS

What's more, the aging university-owned dorms aren't designed to meet the demands of today's college student. Most of the buildings on campus were built in the 1970s and 1980s. The college student of today expects modern residential living with 21st century amenities that include central air-conditioning, high-speed or wireless Internet access, cable TV, fitness centers, in-unit washers and dryers, furnishings, utility packages, dishwashers and garbage disposals, and on-site parking spaces.

As existing public dorm rooms become even older and more obsolete, the demand for well-located student housing with modern amenities will soar—and provide higher rental income than ever before.

INCREASED DEMAND EQUALS GREATER OPPORTUNITIES

In any business, basic economic theory states that when demand increases for a product or service (particularly if the product or service remains in short supply), there will be upward pressure on prices for that product or service.

In residential rental real estate, the principles of supply and demand operate like textbook economics; that is, where a shortage or relatively stable supply of well-located residential rental real estate exists and the number of consumers seeking properties to lease is high, an upward pressure on rental rates will exist. Therefore, under these circumstances, owners can realize a high cash flow from their properties.

As more and more students seek rental housing on university campuses (the inevitable result of current demographic trends), both cash flow and property values increase. Today, the application of simple economics, combined with demographic trends, have resulted in a boom niche opportunity for astute real estate investors!

Given that, the next question becomes: "Where do I invest?"

2

IDENTIFYING PRIME COLLEGE MARKETS

Many believe the key to most good real estate investments remains the old cliché—location, location, location.

Although general demographic trends clearly favor the future prospects of student housing in general (as noted in Chapter 1), one can't simply buy *any* student housing property at *any* location and expect the investment to do well. Aside from requiring the due diligence and underwriting of the specific investment property itself (addressed in later chapters of this book), it's critical to research the state and particular college market thoroughly.

My experience tells me to embrace the location, location, location cliché, *but* I realize that a great location can seductively lead to unreasonable—even disastrous—investment decisions. Overpaying for a piece of real estate in an A+ location will not turn a poor investment into a good one. Similarly, mismanaging a prime location property can be a good way to lose the advantage of an excellent location—and your shirt, too. I'd rather buy a less-than-prime location property for a good deal and a great return any day of the week over a well-located piece of real estate at a purchase price that will never make me money.

That said, I like to increase my chances for success by buying the best location I can for the best deal I can make. I'm also prepared to walk away from making a deal if the price is too high—no matter how great the location. If you are, or become, an active real estate investor and want to be successful at this business, get comfortable with walking away from deals. Don't let a particular location seduce you into making a purchase mistake.

FACTORS FOR CHOOSING THE RIGHT CAMPUS

When it comes to student housing—aside from the fundamentals of the purchase price relative to the projected return—choosing the "right" campus will greatly enhance your odds for a successful investment. Evaluate the following indicators for the student housing investor when identifying campus market opportunities:

- High growth states
- University student housing policy
- Private versus public institutions of higher learning
- Aging student housing stock

HIGH GROWTH STATES

Concentrating your search for student housing investment opportunities in geographic areas that have the greatest potential for enrollment growth will increase your chances for higher returns and appreciation. I call these high growth states. The U.S. Census Bureau has made it easy to pinpoint high growth states by furnishing projections of population growth by age on a state-by-state basis.

The table in Figure 2.1 represents the 20 states that are projected to experience the most significant increases in the target group population between 2000 and 2010.

The government has also made higher education enrollment growth projections. The U.S. Census Bureau estimates the states in Figure 2.2 will have the highest levels of college enrollment growth during the rest of the decade.

FIGURE 2.1 *Population Growth Projections, Ages 18–24*

Rank	State	Change (2000–2010)	Percent Change
1	California	1,196,012 students	38.2%
2	Texas	395,320	18.6
3	New York	302,794	18.6
4	Florida	274,826	21.9
5	Massachusetts	142,520	26.0
6	Georgia	134,177	16.9
7	North Carolina	131,863	18.2
8	Virginia	122,361	18.5
9	New Jersey	105,659	15.1
10	Illinois	97,118	8.3
11	Arizona	96,911	20.8
12	Maryland	94,938	20.3
13	Pennsylvania	85,846	8.1
14	Washington	73,766	13.2
15	Tennessee	55,653	10.2
16	Connecticut	53,506	19.4
17	South Carolina	49,999	13.6
18	Colorado	49,826	12.0
19	Michigan	38,027	4.1
20	Alabama	35,155	8.1

Source: U.S. Census Bureau.

FIGURE 2.2. *Enrollment Growth Projections, 2001–2010*

Rank	State	Change	Percentage Change
1	California	783,020 students	34.0%
2	New York	174,633	16.6
3	Texas	161,494	15.3
4	Florida	131,348	18.2
5	Massachusetts	93,166	21.6
6	North Carolina	62,817	15.3
7	Virginia	61,833	16.0
8	Arizona	57,206	16.2
9	Illinois	50,144	6.7
10	Georgia	48,951	13.9
11	Maryland	47,497	17.1
12	New Jersey	46,459	13.8
13	Pennsylvania	39,318	6.4
14	Washington	34,192	10.5
15	Connecticut	27,816	17.1
16	District of Columbia	27,301	35.9
17	South Carolina	22,713	12.2
18	Colorado	22,707	8.4
19	Tennessee	21,319	8.0
20	Michigan	17,749	3.1

Source: U.S. Census Bureau.

A Few Words of Caution

The use of the population enrollment growth data assists in planning for a student housing investment and aids in searching for properties to acquire. The data cannot, however, be used in a vacuum. Be sure to balance it with the numerous factors discussed throughout this book.

For example, a particular college campus in a state not listed in the top 20 growth states might, in fact, provide a better opportunity than a college campus in California or New York—the top two projected enrollment growth states. I have been researching a $7 million student housing opportunity in Wisconsin, a state that did not even make the list. I'm attracted to this particular Wisconsin campus because it suffers from a student housing shortage. The property is a short walk to the center of campus (it's that location, location, location business again) and has operated at 100 percent occupancy for the last 15 years! I'll take ten deals like this one over any deal near a campus that has too many dorm rooms or an overbuilt off-campus private student housing market—even if it is in a high-growth state.

Key Ratio: University-Owned Housing Beds to Total Enrollment

For my money, the single most important factor in determining a favorable climate for a student housing investment is the ratio of university-owned beds to the total number of enrolled students. The logic is simple: The lower the ratio of beds to students, the greater the need for private-sector student housing.

I acknowledge that it's impossible to simplify a business as complicated as real estate investing and the student housing sector in particular. But if I were forced to choose one, and only one, factor that should be considered when selecting a particular college campus, it would be this one: the university-owned-beds-to-total-enrolled-student ratio.

Demographic trends and university budget constraints work in a real estate investor's favor when it comes to this key ratio. School-owned student housing capacity is, on average nationwide, only 30.12 percent of the total enrolled student population. This means that almost 70 percent of college students must rely on housing alternatives such as living with their parents, purchasing condos/town houses, or renting apartments or houses for a place to live while away at school. As enrollments increase over the next ten years and schools fail to build new dormitories, more students will seek privately owned housing. As student housing real estate investors in the 21st century say, "The trend is our friend."

The table in Figure 2.3 features data based on a survey of each of the 50 states' largest public four-year universities. It indicates the number of school-owned beds and enrolled students along with my calculation of the all-important university-owned-beds-to-enrolled-students ratio. The list shows the lowest, most favorable ratio of beds-to-students in descending order of favorability for the real estate investor.

As valuable as this information can be, it's not the only tool you'll need to make a wise student housing investment decision. After all, this data only covers the largest of the schools in each one of the 50 states. Many states, especially those with large populations, have several large public universities and colleges that have various university-owned-beds-to-student-enrollment ratios worth investigating. In fact, one can argue that much of the coming enrollment growth over the next decade will occur at the second and even third or fourth largest colleges within a given state. And, however crucial, the university-owned-beds-to-enrolled-student ratio doesn't include the all-important local market considerations that will be discussed in Chapter 5, "Finding Student Housing Property Worth Buying."

FIGURE 2.3. *University-Owned-Beds-to-Enrolled-Students Ratio*

		(Largest university in each of the 50 states)		
University Name	**State**	**School-Owned Beds, Fall 2004***	**Enrolled Fall 2004**	**Ratio %**
Boise State University	Idaho	850	18,456	4.60
U. of Alaska–Anchorage	Alaska	950	17,572	5.42
U. of Nevada–Las Vegas	Nevada	1,500	27,000	5.55
Portland State U.	Oregon	1,600	21,348	7.49
U. of New Mexico	New Mexico	2,400	25,031	9.58
Arizona State U.	Arizona	5,600	49,171	11.38
U. of Minnesota–Twin Cities	Minnesota	6,300	50,954	12.36
U. of Maryland–College Park	Maryland	8,700	34,933	12.36

FIGURE 2.3. *University-Owned-Beds-to-Enrolled-Students Ratio*

U. of Texas–Austin	Texas	6,600	52,261	12.62
U. of Washington	Washington	5,000	39,199	12.75
West Virginia U.	West Virginia	3,600	25,255	14.25
U. of Southern Maine	Maine	1,600	11,007	14.53
U. of Hawaii–Manoa	Hawaii	3,000	20,549	14.59
Auburn U.	Alabama	3,400	22,928	14.82
U. of Florida	Florida	7,600	47,000	16.17
U. of Oklahoma	Oklahoma	4,300	24,569	17.50
Ohio State U.	Ohio	9,200	50,995	18.04
U. of Georgia	Georgia	5,800	30,824	18.81
U. of Iowa	Iowa	5,600	29,745	18.82
U. of Kansas	Kansas	5,500	28,849	19.06
U. of California–L.A.	California	7,200	37,563	19.16
U. of Kentucky	Kentucky	5,100	26,545	19.21
U. of Arkansas	Arkansas	3,200	16,461	19.43
Brigham Young U.	Utah	6,500	29,932	21.17
North Carolina State U.	North Carolina	6,700	29,637	22.60
U. of Wyoming	Wyoming	2,800	12,021	23.32
U. of North Dakota	North Dakota	3,200	13,187	24.26
U. of Colorado–Boulder	Colorado	7,100	29,151	24.35
Louisiana State U.	Louisiana	7,600	30,000	25.33
U. of Nebraska–Lincoln	Nebraska	5,600	21,792	25.69
Mississippi State U.	Mississippi	4,000	15,416	25.94
U. of Tennessee	Tennessee	7,300	27,800	26.25
U. of Wisconsin–Madison	Wisconsin	11,000	41,588	26.44
U. of South Carolina	South Carolina	6,800	25,596	26.56
U. of Illinois–Champaign	Illinois	10,855	38,291	28.34
New York U.	New York	11,000	38,188	28.80
Pennsylvania State U.	Pennsylvania	12,000	41,289	29.06
U. of Rhode Island	Rhode Island	3,900	13,435	29.02
South Dakota State U.	South Dakota	3,400	10,954	31.03
U. of Montana–Missoula	Montana	4,500	13,352	33.70
Indiana U.–Bloomington	Indiana	13,000	37,821	34.37
Virginia Tech	Virginia	8,900	25,420	35.01
U. of Delaware	Delaware	7,000	19,418	36.04
Michigan State U.	Michigan	17,000	44,836	37.91
U. of Missouri–Columbia	Missouri	10,000	25,527	39.17
Rutgers, State U. New Jersey	New Jersey	14,000	34,697	40.34
Boston U.	Massachusetts	11,000	26,704	41.19
U. of New Hampshire	New Hampshire	5,500	12,000	45.83
U. of Vermont	Vermont	4,000	9,273	43.13
U. of Connecticut	Connecticut	11,000	23,179	47.45

*Number of beds rounded to the nearest hundred

UNIVERSITY STUDENT HOUSING POLICY

Take time to examine the student housing living policy of the school under consideration for a student housing real estate investment. The policies of universities vary in their requirements for where enrolled students can live. Although notable exceptions exist, most universities require students (at least in their freshman year) to live in university-owned or university-approved dormitories or fraternity and sorority houses on campus. Knowing that makes a difference when identifying a campus that appears favorable to private-sector student housing.

I've observed that most students want to move out of their dorm rooms as soon as they can. Once the school policy allows them to live in private housing, the majority of our future leaders will convince their parents that "everybody" is living in an off-campus rented apartment or house, and that their entire college social life will be ruined if they have to continue living in the dorms. Given this undocumented but typical demographic fact, universities that allow sophomores and upperclassmen to live outside the dorms create a better real estate investment climate for student housing than those that limit off-campus living to upperclassmen and married students.

PRIVATE VERSUS PUBLIC INSTITUTIONS OF HIGHER LEARNING

You may have noticed that I haven't mentioned private colleges and universities when it comes to campus markets of opportunity for student housing. Most successful student housing investors including myself don't see a future in the private college campus market. Private universities tend to apply restrictive requirements on housing and, with a number of exceptions, sometimes even require students to live in the dorms for all four (or increasingly five) years of their higher education.

The culture and social norms at private schools tend to place a great emphasis on students living and collaborating together in dormitories. What's more, the number of enrollees at private institutions has a greater tendency to be capped or severely limited than at public institutions. Public university policies aim to fulfill the obligation of making a college education available to a broad segment of the population, which tends to encourage and guarantee enrollment growth.

While restrictive housing and enrollment policies may be great for keeping the dorm rooms full at private schools, they don't suit your needs as an investor. I hate to say "never" when it comes to real estate investing; I even spend time looking at almost any student housing deal before I say "No thanks." But in my experience, I will say "almost never" does a private college student housing deal make sense because the schools themselves usually have plenty of dorm rooms and they impose restrictive housing and enrollment policies on their students.

AGING STUDENT HOUSING STOCK

The quality of the university-owned dorm room "competition" for students seeking housing varies from campus to campus. As consumers in general—and students seeking housing in particular—become more demanding, the age of buildings and amenities provided by university-owned dorms becomes an increasingly important factor. Most aging college dormitories have become functionally obsolete. On some college campuses, dorm rooms don't have air-conditioning or adequate lighting and ventilation. They almost never have enough storage and laundry space. And given ongoing state budget constraints, it is highly unlikely the universities will take on major rehabilitation for these buildings any time soon.

Many schools continue to struggle with funding, causing an even greater reliance on—and competitive advantage for—the private student housing alternative. In several cases, the costs of required rehabilitation—including new mechanical systems, roofs, and mandated life safety changes—are so prohibitive that universities have taken complete dormitory buildings out of service and thus decreased the supply.

Managers of out-of-date and amenity-deficient school-owned dorms find it increasingly difficult to compete with private bathrooms, luxury kitchens, cable television packages, and high-speed Internet connections offered by the private student housing sector. Therefore, when evaluating a particular college campus, you increase your odds for success and rental revenue growth by selecting campuses where dorms are outdated and sorely need renovating. If you're considering investing near those rare campuses that are upgrading and renovating their dorms, I urge caution. Do your homework thoroughly before making a real estate housing investment in those communities.

BENEFIT FROM HIGH OCCUPANCY LEVELS

Despite various caveats and cautionary words, most public universities tend to show a highly favorable environment for private student housing investment. The school-owned-beds-to-enrolled-students data *at the current numbers* point to a favorable investment environment at each of the largest public universities in every state in the union. Given the unstoppable enrollment growth on the way and the projected flat or small growth of university-owned beds, the ratios go only in one direction—toward an even lower percentage of university-owned beds to serve the increased numbers of students seeking college degrees.

As this trend continues into the next decade and beyond, a nationwide student housing shortage is pending. In the course of my real estate investment business, I have had the opportunity to examine rent rolls and income and expense statements on hundreds, perhaps thousands, of real estate investments. I have never seen lower vacancy rates and higher occupancy levels in any sector (other than entire buildings leased long-term to a single tenant) than I routinely see in student housing properties. Occupancy levels far above that of traditional residential rental real estate investments is the norm in the student housing niche.

What's more, student housing occupancy levels align with the demand by students for housing at their college campuses. History has shown that enrollments aren't tied to external economic factors such as job growth and interest rates. Rather, they're tied to the size of the population that is graduating from high school and turning to college—a constantly growing number as noted in Chapter 1. The demand for student housing increases as that population number goes up. As a result, occupancy levels of 97 percent to 100 percent for many years are *already* common in the student housing market.

STILL ROOM FOR ENTREPRENEURS AND INDEPENDENT INVESTORS

Unlike other areas of investment opportunity with strong future prospects, the student housing niche market in particular has been dominated by entrepreneurs and individual independent investors. To be sure, the large institutional investors and recent initial public offerings (IPOs) for new real estate investment trusts (REITs) have brought large amounts of corporate and Wall Street capital into student housing. This niche, however, still largely remains the domain of individual private investors.

Did you notice that no big chain national firms like Hyatt, Marriott, or Starwood control the student housing market or even have a presence? As with traditional multifamily residential apartment rental properties, the ownership of student housing assets is highly fragmented. While the total demand for student housing is well over ten million units nationwide, no single firm or individual investor group controls in excess of 25,000 student housing rental units. There are currently only eight top firms nationwide in the business, with student housing beds of 10,000 to 25,000 units per firm under management. Not one single firm or person in this business controls close to 0.5 percent market share! In fact, the top eight largest firms control less than 2 percent of the private student housing market combined! (This data was compiled from the Securities and Exchange Commission IPO filing of GMH Communities Trust in October of 2004.)

Where Large Players Purchase

To date, the larger national firms have focused their efforts on states that have large statewide university systems and solid prospects for large increases in enrollments. The big firms have wanted to own and manage clusters of multiple student housing properties within the same states to take advantage of management economies of scale. As a result, the dominant big players (if less than a 2 percent market share can be called "big") have tended to purchase and build student housing properties in the states of Texas, California, Florida, Georgia, North Carolina, Arizona, and Pennsylvania.

I don't shy away from a little competition, but if I have a choice to go up against someone with $200 million in cost-free IPO money or another private investor, I'll stay away from the players who have that IPO money burning holes in their pockets. As a result, unless a deal is small enough that the big boys won't look at it, I stay away from student housing transaction in the states where they're gathering steam by purchasing student housing assets in large numbers.

Sure, enough colleges and universities have an adequate supply of school-owned housing, but the high growth states will keep individual or entrepreneurial group investors in the money. That way, they can avoid engaging in a competition that's difficult to win. Additionally, enough small below-the-radar-screen deals exist. With less than than $1 million at the largest university systems, you can head for high growth states without running up against the big deep-pocketed guys.

Don't Get Scared Off

Please don't let my definition of small deals scare you off. You'll discover lots of ways to get started and make profits in the student housing real estate market niche conducting deals as small as $100,000. By starting out with limited equity, you can quickly become capable of making a $5 million+ deal. (You'll find details of various sources and techniques for raising equity and building a large student housing property portfolio in Part Two of this book.)

It is time to get in the game and buy something, then accumulate a student housing portfolio that will make money and appreciate in value. Part Two discusses the three key ingredients you will need to "do the deal" in your own way: equity, debt financing, and property worth buying.

EQUITY, DEBT FINANCING, AND PROPERTY WORTH BUYING

Clearly, the student housing market niche is unique. If you want to enter the student housing market, it would be wise to understand the potential pitfalls of rental properties on college campuses.

Many factors affect the viability of a student housing investment that don't apply to traditional residential investment real estate properties. For example, additional management and operational issues in this niche require the attention and diligence of the investor both *before* and especially *after* the property is acquired.

While student housing investments have their distinctions, I've also found similarities to acquiring all types of real estate investments. If you're new to investing or you're a seasoned investor managing large real estate portfolios, you're wise to master three key areas to close the purchase of any real estate investment transaction. I hate to oversimplify—to be sure, many details require your attention in getting a real estate deal closed—but the three recurring key aspects in any investment property acquisition are:

1. Having equity to invest
2. Arranging financing
3. Finding property worth buying

Three areas are so fundamentally important that each warrants its own chapter. Here's what you can expect as you read on:

The seasoned investor will find the information in Chapter 3, the equity chapter, somewhat basic and perhaps unnecessary but it's excellent for new investors. Chapter 4, the financing chapter, describes potential sources of financing that specialize in the student housing niche. These provide new resources for experienced and inexperienced investors alike. Chapter 5 on finding student housing property worth buying is a "must" read for investors at any level of experience because of this niche's unique nature.

Once you've learned to master and control these three areas, you can greatly increase your potential for success and increased wealth! Read on.

3

EQUITY: WHAT IT IS AND HOW TO GET IT

When I started investing, I had the lucky advantage of being the third generation in my family to enter the business of buying and owning real estate. Through family partnerships and investments as well as a salary from the family business, I had a fabulous head start. That meant I already had money available to make my own investments. Along the way, the sale of properties that appreciated in value gave me even more available equity so I could increase the size of my investment portfolio and grow my net worth.

If you have access to family wealth, I suggest you use it to build a strong real estate investment portfolio that will increase your own financial security and provide for generations of your family to come. Having a head start gives you a distinct advantage over those looking for equity to make investments. By investing money prudently, you build on the luck of being born into the right family and the satisfaction of making your own mark.

YOU DON'T HAVE TO COME FROM WEALTH

Yet, even if you weren't born with a silver spoon, you can still be radically successful in real estate. Many people who are now multimillion-dollar real estate entrepreneurs came from ordinary families and started with absolutely nothing. Several others have lost fortunes in their careers and businesses, but made huge financial comebacks in the real estate investment business.

Clearly, the real estate investment field offers anybody with ambition the ability to get a second (sometimes a third) chance to achieve financial independence and accumulate wealth. I know of no other business that has created as many individual entrepreneur millionaires who started with nothing. In any town, the single largest contributor to the net worth of the wealthiest people is most often the value of their real estate holdings. And when successful family businesses are sold, usually the appreciated value of the company-owned real estate holdings provides their greatest value—more than the operating businesses themselves.

WHAT IS EQUITY?

Have you heard about the "no money down" seminars or read "how to" books for beginning real estate investors? Bookstore shelves and cable television channels have no shortage of "no money down" real estate investment hawkers. Infomercials, seminars at local hotels, and product offerings abound. The hawkers usually promise to turn their buyers into millionaires in a short time by teaching them the secrets of "no money down" real estate investing. The only catch to learning these "secret" techniques is to pay the authors or seminar leaders their fees, up front of course.

Why are these promoters spending so much time holding seminars and producing infomercials instead of buying real estate without money? Perhaps it's because they make more money in seminar fees and book royalties than in practicing the techniques they teach!

Here's my take on this: I have been at this business a long time as a third-generation real estate investor. I've served in many leadership positions including the board of directors of a major real estate association. I've also served on a bank's board of directors and loan committees, and I've personally known successful real estate investors. I may have overlooked a "secret" real estate investment technique over the years, but I doubt it. Let me be 100 percent crystal clear on this point—*I have never known or seen a real estate investor who has built a multimillion-dollar real estate portfolio without hard equity money invested in properties.*

Hard Money

Equity is the actual hard money that needs to be invested in a real estate transaction to obtain financing and close a deal. Generally, in the multifamily residential real estate field, the required equity investment equals 20 percent to 25 percent of the purchase price of the property.

What's the quickest, easiest way to obtain equity and purchase a piece of property? Simply write a check. However, if you don't have enough cash to provide the equity for a transaction, don't get discouraged and stop reading this book. My lack of confidence in the "no money down" promoters doesn't mean that your equity must come from your own bank balance. If you have the money to make the investment and all of the other pieces can fit together, you still may want a partner.

Partnership Arrangement

Remember, the real estate business is replete with people who have built up a large net worth even though they started with little or no money of their own. If you can master the other two key areas for creating a real estate deal—arranging financing and finding property worth buying—you can structure a joint venture or partnership to obtain the required equity and close the deal. Before you decide that you don't have the equity money available yourself to make the investment, make sure you really don't have hidden equity available. Consider the potential sources of equity you may already have.

POTENTIAL SOURCES OF EQUITY

Most people who have owned a residence for any length of time have realized an appreciation value in their homes. By tapping into this appreciation value with a home equity loan—the easiest type of financing to obtain—you have cash available to provide the equity for a property purchase. Or by partnering with a friend or business associate who also has home equity available for investing, potentially you could invest in larger and more numerous investments, too.

Many successful investors, myself included, have used home equity loans to establish lines of credit, which provide liquidity and equity when needed to purchase real estate investment properties. Bankers love making home equity loans and, because of the low default rate and potential to grow more customer relationships, they often make interest rates and terms the most attractive of any loan their banks offer.

In fact, even if you don't have an immediate need, setting up a home equity line of credit gives you a low-cost method of creating available equity "firepower" when an opportunity presents itself. Lining up potential equity requirements before an actual real estate investment deal comes your way can give you the confidence and ability to move decisively at the right time.

Borrow on Margin from a Brokerage Account

Depending on your tolerance for risk, another potential source of real estate investment equity is borrowing on margin from a brokerage account. Assuming that you have a brokerage account with a good-size portfolio of stocks and bonds that you've set up as a margin account, you can draw down a portion of its value, then use the cash for equity in a real estate transaction.

I am a firm believer that if you're serious about the real estate investment business, you should have at your fingertips as much equity firepower as possible. So look for ways to have sources like brokerage accounts at your disposal and be ready with funds in case an opportunity to buy the right property comes around.

Life Insurance Policies

Whole life insurance policies are another potential source of equity firepower. Most whole life policies have a feature that allows the owner to take out a loan against the paid-in cash surrender value of the policy. Rates of interest are generally low, but the loan will reduce the amount of the death benefit payout. Taking out a loan on a whole life policy is a tax-free way to raise money for a real estate investment and make a potential property acquisition come together. As long as the policyholder remains current on making minimum interest payments annually, loans against cash surrender values of life insurance policies never have to be repaid.

Credit Card Lines of Credit

If you have an extremely high tolerance for risk and an appetite for high-cost equity, credit card lines of credit can be another source of equity for real estate property investments (though I strongly recommend against doing this).

Yes, I do know a few successful investors who tapped credit card cash advance checks to invest in real estate and started their careers that way. I even know of one investor—one of the smartest people I've met in business—who once used credit card cash advances to pay rent for a downtown Chicago LaSalle Street office. Through that office, he attracted institutional and investor equity money to manage and invest in real estate and venture capital transactions. Today, that investor's net worth exceeds $75 million. He owns a controlling interest in a publicly traded company, and, I am certain, carries no monthly balance on his VISA card!

THE PARTNER ADVANTAGE

If you want to purchase investment real estate but don't have the required amount of equity money available yourself—or you simply want to share the risk (and reward) of a real estate investment with others—consider taking in partners or forming a joint venture.

I am a fan of having active *operating* partners in the real estate business. Knowing that few people are competent in every aspect of running a real estate investment business, I believe bringing in partners with strengths that complement your areas of weakness can be of great value. Even if you have enough equity to complete your initial few acquisitions and want to grow the size of your portfolio, you'll need to fund future transactions as well. Sooner or later, you could run out of equity steam. Bringing in partners—especially if they have wealth—can boost your ability to build a real estate investment property portfolio. That's how to super-charge the growth of a real estate empire and each partner's net worth.

"Fall in Love" with a Rich Partner

I see no shame in making money and no reason to disguise your moneymaking motives when pursuing a real estate investment opportunity. To paraphrase a cliché about a materialistic marriage: "When it comes to partners in real estate, why not fall in love with a rich partner instead of a poor one?"

It's important to attract a partner who brings a complementary skill set to the table. I recommend selecting partners who have money to bring to the relationship. Remember this: Bringing in partners without money doesn't help you find the equity for purchasing a piece of real estate, but it will cost you a share of the profits and appreciation anyway.

My Own Partner

My business partner is wealthy, smart, highly educated, and better at details, operations, and management than I am. By pooling our talents, collective net worths, and available equity, we have a greater real estate asset value than I could have accumulated on my own. Another advantage: my partner is a woman, Barbara Gaffen. Unlike the residential sales side of the real estate business, the real estate investment and acquisition sector of real estate is dominated by men. Even in the 21st century, women are rarely seen at the negotiating table as principals in commercial real estate transactions. A relatively low number of women are among the ranks of commercial brokerage personnel. Women seem to have made their largest showing of equality on the legal side of the business. In fact, I have noticed that the number of female commercial and investment real estate attorneys involved in transactions I'm part of is increasing. As a result, women who are active in the real estate investment and acquisition industry get noticed.

Use Your Wealth Wisely

Life can be highly rewarding when you collaborate with other people in a common effort that doesn't include money. But unlike aspects of my life that involve helping the community and people less fortunate than me, cash is indeed king when it comes to the real estate business. Keep that in mind.

I believe this business should be practiced in a principled and ethical way. Also keep in mind that your goal is to make money and build wealth, not to save the world. I hope you use the wealth you build to provide for yourselves and your families as well as contribute to worthy causes that make the world a better place!

I encourage aspiring female entrepreneurs to enter this wide-open field. If you are a woman hanging with a crowd of guys, you'll likely receive welcome access to deals and major transactions. I have not seen widespread evidence of discrimination against women preventing them from advancing in the field; rather, I think the low number of women in commercial real estate carries over from years of stereotyping a few suitable careers for females. None of those stereotypical careers included real estate investing!

OTHER SOURCES OF EQUITY

Aside from your own money and the funds from your active business partner, you can turn to other sources of equity to fund your start-up real estate investment enterprise or provide for the growth of an existing operation. These include:

- Friends and relatives
- Joint ventures
- Syndications
- Institutional partners

Friends and Relatives

Relatives and close friends can be excellent sources of initial equity, particularly for novices getting started in real estate investing. Most people have one or two friends or relatives (or even a greater number) who have money to invest in a real estate transaction. By identifying an opportunity to acquire, doing the legwork, and crunching the numbers, the aspiring real estate entrepreneur can impress friends or relatives, making them inclined to become investors. If you get turned down, don't be a pest, but be persistent and find other potential investors.

When seeking investors, remember that people who are affluent like to invest their money but often have a problem finding opportunities in which to invest their money. By partnering with them, you can actually help solve the problem of how to invest their extra money. If you can show them your competence at identifying

Covering Grandma's Interest

A friend of mine, a real estate broker, had little money of his own. One day, he spotted a well-located three-flat apartment building in need of rehab—a diamond in the rough. He went to visit his grandma, a lifelong saver, about being an investor in this project. But when she learned that she had to wait for the complete rehab and resale of the property to see her return on investment, Grandma turned him down flat.

As it turned out, she needed the interest earned on her savings each month to live on. So my friend came back to Grandma and offered to pay her the equivalent of six months' worth of interest up front (a payment he could manage from his meager checking account balance). After agreeing to that, she jumped at the chance to help her grandson get started. A few months later when the property was resold, Grandma made a large return on her investment. My friend built an investment and building career that has won numerous development awards. He also served as president of his local homebuilders association and, by the way, became a multimillionaire.

and managing real estate investment opportunities, you will raise the equity you need to complete the deal through their participation.

As the buzz spreads within your circle about initial successes, watch for results to snowball. Other family members and friends will want a piece of your action. When that happens, you'll have more sources of equity to conduct more deals through their equity.

Many large real estate portfolios are owned entirely by groups of family members and friends of the initial deal promoter. Depending on the amount of available wealth within your own circle, once you get momentum, you will rarely have to go outside of your circle to find the equity you need.

Joint Ventures

Unlike direct partnerships in an operating real estate investment business, joint ventures can be excellent ways to lower risk and share in the required equity for a single real estate investment or a group of real estate investments.

With joint venture strategic alliances with a firm or individual, real estate entrepreneurs can take on larger transactions or more rapid growth than by staying independent. By combining forces, all joint venture partners share in the risk as well as the rewards while each contributes only a portion of the equity needed.

When my partner and I decided to jump into the student housing real estate niche, we knew we were faced with a great opportunity for future appreciation. We wanted to make as many prudent acquisitions as we could reasonably handle, so we formed a strategic alliance with a well-capitalized and highly respected joint venture partner, then looked at student housing deals together. Although that meant giving up half of the cash flow and upside appreciation, we're getting an extra set of professional evaluation eyes and lots of equity firepower we'd never have on our own. And because we want to load up on student housing, we

> **Choose the Right Joint Venture Partner**
>
> As with operating partners, selecting the right joint venture partner is key. I am fortunate to joint venture with a "prince" of a partner. We trust each other and work well together. I wouldn't have it any other way; it's not worth giving up half the deal to a joint venture partner who is difficult to work with or doesn't carry a fair share of the workload.

made a strategic decision to give up half of the ownership interest in the deals so we could deepen our pockets and double our available equity for investing.

Syndications

Yet another excellent source of equity is through a syndication of a number of passive investor partners. Syndications, which usually take the legal form of limited partnerships or limited liability companies, are used for transactions requiring large amounts of equity. Once a track record has been established, syndications can be excellent sources of equity from high-net-worth individual investors seeking to invest a portion of their assets in real estate.

If you've never syndicated a deal, it is wise to keep a list of potential passive investors in case you choose to syndicate one in the future. As anyone in the real estate investment business can confirm, friends, relatives, contacts, and acquaintances seeking investment opportunities often inquire about bringing outside investors into your real estate transactions. The more successful and visible you become, the greater the number of potential syndication contacts you'll have for your list.

The legal requirements, disclosures, and documentation required to raise equity money through syndications are regulated and highly technical. You'll require experienced and prudent legal counsel to properly prepare the offering memoranda and required disclosures. *Do not skimp on this or take shortcuts.* If you violate the rules, you'll face serious legal consequences.

However, if the deal is large enough and the target group of investors has an appetite for it, syndications can raise large sums of equity capital to make acquisitions and fund the growth of a large real estate portfolio.

You'll find that syndications have their downside. Once you've plunged in and crossed over from using either your own money or money from a small group of friends and relatives, you've entered the world of being accountable to outside partners. Real estate deals rarely work out exactly as projected. Outside investors who have entrusted their money with you have the right to receive reports on the progress of their investment, including periodic financial statements.

Sometimes you have to share bad news with a large group of people who would not be privy to knowing the issues (or mistakes) in your real estate deals if they were not your partners. My experience indicates that sophisticated investors in syndications can take the news—good or bad—as long as it's presented early and in a clear and concise manner. In the long run, most real estate deals work out fine and investors end up happy and confident—as long as they're kept informed.

Be extremely selective in choosing investors for syndications. I have learned not to solicit money or accept subscriptions for partnership units from difficult people or anyone counting on rapid returns of invested funds. These types of investors are simply not worth the almost certain aggravation they will cause. Instead, ideal candidates for real estate investment syndications are high-net-worth investors who seek to invest a small portion of their wealth in real estate. They have outside sources of income and can handle the possibility of receiving no distributions from time to time if available cash needs to be reinvested in the building.

Get on a Syndication Bandwagon

With our student housing portfolio acquisitions, our combined entity is using limited liability company syndications to raise millions of dollars in equity capital. If the deal is sound and the promoting partners have the necessary track record and knowledge, large amounts of passive investor money can be available to provide equity for continued acquisitions. We see how investor confidence increases when we put our own hard equity money into each deal. Once you use this syndication method for raising equity successfully, subsequent deals sell out quickly. Naturally, potential investors want to get on a winning bandwagon.

Institutional Partners

Institutional investing represents the major leagues of the real estate investment business; there's no quicker way to enter the realm of multimillion-dollar deals and build major real estate empires. Institutional investors include insurance companies, pension funds, and aggregated institutional investor pooled investment funds.

Many institutional investors seek to enter joint ventures with well-established, experienced real estate entrepreneurs for large student housing deals exceeding $10 million in acquisition price. Large institutions allocate a portion of their massive assets—billions of dollars a year—for investments in the real estate sector. Because large institutions have little operating and asset management internal abilities, their decision makers rarely (if ever) buy real estate without joint venture operating partners.

These investors are aware of the positive demographic trends pointing to excellent future prospects through well-located student housing investments. And they eagerly review proposals for investing their allocated billions into real estate deals.

Investment property portfolios valued in the hundreds of millions to billions of dollars have been built by real estate entrepreneurs using institutional investor money. Having one investor to talk to (instead of the many individual passive partners required in individual investor syndication) is easier and more efficient when putting together a large transaction. Additionally, in the student housing niche, institutional investors regularly place up to 90 percent of the equity required for the transaction. This limits the promoting real estate investor's equity to 10 percent of the total required. With institutional money to back you up, your own available equity will last much longer while giving you control of substantial amounts of student housing assets.

What It Means to Be Part of This Club

Making the decision to go the institutional investor route sounds alluring. It's definitely an exclusive club that will place you in great company. Entry into this club is limited to those with a proven track record. That means you must have actual transactions under contract that can be underwritten to show high returns using rigorous standards.

Institutional investors tend to dictate "take it or leave it" terms. Preferred returns to the institution are high, combined with minimum rates of return required and short-time exit strategies. Because most of the return on a real estate investment is realized when a property is sold and institutions have stringent rate-of-return benchmarks, to hit the required rate, properties usually must be sold within a five-year time frame. Investors can't hold a property longer if the cash flow is good and future prospects are bright, considering that the institutional investor with a 90 percent equity interest calls the shots.

Additionally, institutional investors retain the right to toss you and your management out of the deal if they are unhappy with the returns. Unlike dealing with limited partnerships or limited liability company syndications, when dealing with institutional money, you are in control of the deal only as long as you can hit (or exceed) the projections.

EQUITY ALWAYS AVAILABLE FOR GOOD DEEDS

Given the number of potential sources of equity available to astute real estate entrepreneurs, finding equity should never be a stumbling block to closing a good real estate deal.

If you have a well-located, high-occupancy student housing deal under contract and you can't get the equity together to close on the transaction, something must be wrong with the deal. If so, make sure you're not overpaying for the property and start looking for a way out of the contract. Most likely, you've made a serious mistake.

4

DEBT FINANCING STUDENT HOUSING

Once you have the equity required for the down payment on a transaction, you can raise the remainder of the purchase price by mortgaging the property to a lending source. While some investors choose to place large amounts of equity into deals and limit the amount they finance, most investors seek to minimize the amount of equity placed in each deal. They prefer to keep their hard cash available as equity for future transactions.

GET AGGRESSIVE WHEN USING FINANCING

Although my partner and I tend to be conservative in the way we underwrite and calculate potential cash flow on real estate deals, we get aggressive when it comes to using financing. More often than not, we mortgage a property as much as we comfortably can. That said, we never put ourselves at risk of being short on cash flow to cover expenses and fund a contingency reserve (as well as pay the mortgage). But we like to save as much equity firepower as possible for the next deal.

A serious real estate investor always looks to the next, not yet identified, acquisition. We "deal junkies" secretly suffer from the un-founded fear that we won't have enough money for that impossible-to-pass-up bargain purchase about to cross our desk next month!

Lenders can be a great tonic for this until-now private phobia shared by real estate entrepreneurs. On good real estate deals with conservative projections, lenders want you to borrow as much as they can lend within acceptable loan guidelines. It's not a mystery why this is so; the more you borrow, the more they earn in fees and interest. In fact, on many occasions, I have found hungry lenders willing to finance transactions we have passed on because other buyers relied on unrealistic broker projections and were willing to overpay.

Most student housing real estate acquisitions as well as apartment property transactions are eligible for between 75 percent and 80 percent mortgage financing. To close the transaction and complete the acquisition (after the equity is raised), 75 percent to 80 percent comes from placing debt on the property to be acquired. Student housing properties are included in that. Here's the good news. Because of the growing popularity of this niche

Don't Rely on Lender's Approval to Judge a Deal

Here's my word of caution: When financing a transaction, it's a mistake to rely on a lender's approval of enough funds. I believe doing so is truly a disaster waiting to happen. Particularly in low-interest environments, lenders who eagerly put out lots of money in commercial and investment real estate loans can get too loose with their checkbooks. Be careful; it's tempting to omit doing your own due diligence, then getting into an undesirable property simply because the money is so easy to obtain. You might get stuck with a property that has high costs and low income. Remember, lenders aren't looking out for your interests; they care about lending money!

among lenders, potential additional sources of financing have become available to investors at attractive rates.

LENDER RELATIONS

The real estate investment business—more than any business I can think of—is based on forming relationships. Serious investors are never onetime buyers, which makes it even more crucial to build strong relationships.

Unlike a family buying a home once or twice in a lifetime, serious investors growing property portfolios engage in many transactions over the course of their careers. Arranging financing to purchase a principal residence requires almost none of the same skills as arranging for a mortgage on an investment property. There is much more to an investment property financing transaction than meets the eye.

I can't overstate the importance of building strong, long-term relationships as a key ingredient to succeed in real estate investing, particularly in this niche. Specifically, there is no greater asset or resource you can cultivate and maintain than ongoing relationships with sources of financing. With mortgage financing representing 75 percent to 80 percent of the money needed to close a deal, the financing terms can make or break the economic viability of a deal. Quick and efficient access to that mortgage financing is fundamental to succeeding in this business. Indeed, without the use of mortgage financing, you have no real estate investment business.

Importance of Leverage

Financing—called "leverage" in the industry—gives you the financial ability to acquire large amounts of real estate and enhance your overall return on equity.

"Leverage" is to "investment real estate" as "water" is to "fish." If you are in the real estate investment business, you can't make money and grow your portfolio without using leverage. Not surprisingly, the best real estate entrepreneurs and creators of the most wealth tend to have excellent lender relationships and access to the best financing terms available.

When several potential buyers compete for a prime piece of real estate, those who have lined up their financing in advance

Lining Up Quick Financing

A few years ago, I was forced to develop a "no mortgage contingency" method of making offers, even on large transactions. This evolved from having to compete for apartment property acquisition deals in hot Chicago neighborhoods where we (and just about everyone else) have been hungry for condominium conversions. At this stage in my career, I simply don't need to make my offers contingent on getting a mortgage. Why? Because I line up my financing in advance by tapping into my established, informed network of commercial real estate mortgage sources.

My partner and I take pride in the long-standing relationships we've cultivated with local and national banks as well as commercial mortgage brokers. We talk to our bankers frequently, even when we don't have a particular deal under contract. We add lenders and potential new leverage sources soliciting our business to our database for mailings and updates on the status of our business. At least twice a year, we mail information to those on our lenders' database. For example, we'd send a reprint of an article featuring our company or an announcement of a recent acquisition.

In an attempt to keep our lending rates and terms as attractive as possible, we let our sources know that we deal with multiple sources of financing. We also share the details of transactions with those lenders who did not finance a particular acquisition. That way, they become aware of our activities and realize that they don't have an exclusive on our business. We also facilitate networking with lending sources through our involvement in associations, commitments to civic activities, and membership in chambers of commerce (and similar organizations).

can outmaneuver their competitors by confidently tying up the property early in the process. When I compete with other buyers for a property (a process I prefer to avoid, but unfortunately I often face), I like to stand out from the crowd and make aggressively strong offers. These offers involve more than price. They include three elements: (1) larger-than-typical earnest money deposits, (2) shorter due diligence times (more on due diligence in the next chapter), and (3) no mortgage contingency. These elements get the sellers' attention fast.

Cultivate Lender Relationships

When bankers or other potential lending sources ask me what is new, I take the time to bring them into the process early—and in confidence—on potential acquisitions. I carefully and methodically set them up to *want* to give me millions of dollars for my yet-unknown next deal. For example, by the time our firm decided to enter the student housing real estate niche, our current lenders and potential additional sources knew about our plans. They were eager to look at our acquisitions right from the start.

As you carry out more deals and become more visible in the investment real estate community, you'll find that bankers seek you out. They want to hear about your business plans. I suggest you use your downtime to cultivate lender relationships. That way, you set the stage for quick and positive answers to your future mortgage financing requests.

Do you see that through established relationships with lenders, you can prime the pump and get your student housing niche mortgage financing source network in place before you ever set foot on a college campus?

MULTIPLE SOURCES OF FINANCING

The widespread appetite for student housing deals in the lending community offers further evidence of excellent growth prospects for this category of real estate. The increased availability of mortgage financing serves as a vote of confidence in this niche, giving investors like you greater incentive to commit to this field.

If you are seeking mortgage financing on a well-located, high-occupancy, student housing deal, I'd say you're in good shape. Experienced lending sources look favorably on traditional multi-family apartment property transactions; they love and offer even more attractive financing on student housing deals!

Traditional Bank Financing

Residential investment property mortgage loans have long been a preferred product category for both national and local banks that have established commercial real estate lending departments. Banks already active in making real estate loans are receptive to looking at additional opportunities. If they understand the market, most are highly receptive to the student housing market. Local branches of national banking organizations and community banks located in college towns understand this market especially well. Therefore, they can be excellent sources for local property mortgage financing. Because banks are under regulatory pressure to make loans within their local designated credit markets, branches of national bank organizations are particularly receptive to making local real estate loans.

For seasoned real estate investors entering the student housing niche, existing bank sources of financing can also be excellent sources. If your own banks have a track record of positive experience with you—and you can show you're familiar with the positive prospects in this niche—you'll find that they welcome the opportunity for increased business. When you present the details of the proposed student housing transaction, sharing the positive demographic trends described in this book will help you get a positive response. Especially for your initial deals, you'll see that it's much easier to deal with a banking relationship you've cultivated than start from scratch with a new source.

Working with Small Banks

I enjoy my relationships with smaller community and regional banks as well as national players. Small local and regional banks offer quick approvals, continuity of bank personnel, and ease of documentation in getting a transaction closed. As your investment property portfolio grows, however, using these banks exclusively can become a barrier because of their legal lending limits, which are smaller than those of large banks. Despite the excellent performance of your loans, at some point in the growth of your real estate portfolio, local and regional banks will reach their legal lending ceiling. The solution? Use multiple local and regional banks or establish a relationship with one or more large banking companies. With large regional and national banks, you'll have unlimited lending capacity as well as a wider variety of mortgage loan products often unavailable from small institutions. In fact, a large bank can even offer credit terms at interest rates on loans that are tied to LIBOR, T-bills, or other indexes. That can result in lower mortgage interest rate terms.

Working with Large Banks

On the downside, large banks have a habit of creating too much red tape to complete real estate transactions and approve loan funding. Unlike the "on-the-phone first-call approvals" you have come to love at your local community banks, national banks need formal approval from various committees before answering "Yes."

In addition, because of consolidations, mergers, and promotions within the national banking organizations, lending officers are constantly being moved to new assignments. (I have not used a local college town branch of a large national bank for a loan transaction yet, but I'm told they have much less employee turnover and more continuity than I've experienced with national banks in the Chicago area.)

RECOURSE FINANCING

Traditional bank mortgage financing from local and regional banks is almost always perceived as a negative because their financing on commercial real estate loans (including student housing deals) is full recourse financing.

Recourse financing, compared with a nonrecourse loan, requires the personal guarantee of the borrowing entity's individual principals. That means even though the property may be purchased by a limited liability company or limited partnership, you can expect to personally guarantee any deficiency on the mortgage loan in the event the investment doesn't work out and a deficiency balance owed to the bank exists after liquidation.

In most cases, only the active operating partners are required to personally guarantee the mortgage loan. Passive investors (those involved when using syndications) are generally not required to personally guarantee mortgage loans covering the investment property. Indeed, requiring a personal recourse guarantee for passive investors would make raising equity by the syndication method impossible.

My View on Personal Guarantees

I am not so adverse as other investors to the principle of recourse financing and personal guarantees. Frankly, I don't like having to add up my total contingent liability obligations under personal guarantees covering recourse loans in our real estate portfolio, but I am comfortable with the risk. Many seasoned investors I respect strongly disagree with my stance. But I have been at this a long time and have *never once* had to come up with money on an investment as a result of a personal guarantee. I conclude that the likelihood of my personal guarantee being required is so remote that I'm not concerned.

My anecdote to recourse financing with a personal guarantee is to take extra care with the underwriting and risk analysis of all potential acquisitions. That way, I sleep well at night. In addition, we always put enough equity into the deal, making the real risk of a future deficiency above the loan balance remote. If our projections for the deal don't indicate enough cash flow (i.e., there's inadequate coverage for anticipated expenses, reasonable reserves, and loan payments due the bank), I don't push the deal. I prefer to walk away if I can't buy the property at a price that gives me positive cash flow.

Requires Discipline and Training

Yes, you'll find it tough to walk away from a well-located, high-occupancy student housing property when you get as excited about the overall potential market as I am. It takes discipline and training, but that's what you need to survive in the real estate investment business. I don't rely on rosy projections from brokers or encouraging advice from bankers eager to book another loan. I buy into an old but not overused cliché in this business: "Don't fall in love with a building." Live by those words and you will stay out of financial trouble.

No matter what type of financing my partner and I are considering, we've found a growing number of nonrecourse lending sources available in the student housing niche. Ironically, as in all investment real estate transactions, the larger the transaction, the more numerous the potential sources of nonrecourse financing for the deal. For example, as the student housing asset class has grown in acceptance and desirability within the lending community, several sources offering financing without personal guarantees have entered the market. Even though successful real estate investors often refuse to sign personal guarantees and only use nonrecourse financing, novice investors will find getting loans difficult until they establish a record of success. Because of the additional burden of paperwork, red tape, and significantly higher costs, I suggest using nonrecourse lending sources only for large multifamily student housing transactions that exceed $3 million.

Although it's theoretically possible to contact nonrecourse financing sources directly, I don't advise doing it. Once you've established a track record and have a few deals under your belt, set up a relationship with good commercial mortgage bankers from the ranks of national commercial mortgage loan companies as well as respected regional firms. When conducting your due diligence, make sure they have vast experience and many contacts with commercial real estate loan sources.

BROKERS AS SOURCES FOR LEADS

Commercial mortgage brokers can also be excellent sources for potential property leads. Well-connected brokers have vast contacts within the investment ownership and brokerage community, and will often hear about opportunities before they're fully exposed to the market. By educating mortgage brokers on your acquisition criteria, you'll have knowledgeable and well-connected sources of potential deals on your team. Commercial mortgage brokers are not compensated by the hour or retainer; they earn their fees out of the origination fees charged for making the loan.

That makes them inexpensive allies to stay in contact with. Your only cost comes out of the closing origination fees once you've closed on a proposed loan.

Remember, the goal of commercial mortgage brokers is to help you structure a financing transaction at the best possible rate. They want you to close on a loan through them so they can earn a fee from placing the mortgage—and impress you for the next opportunity.

Don't make the mistake of using a residential home loan mortgage broker who claims to have contacts with commercial and investment real estate lending sources. Check out the person's track record and types of recent transactions actually closed by the potential mortgage brokerage firm you are dealing with. It's to your advantage to retain a mortgage brokerage firm that has extensive experience in student housing transactions. That way, you can avoid a steep learning curve and enjoy the benefits of knowing the best financing sources for your niche.

Hire Brokers with Various Funding Sources

Although I am always a proponent of working with the right individual regardless of firm affiliation, in this area of commercial real estate, be sure to hire the right individual at the right commercial mortgage banking firm. Commercial mortgage brokers are only as good as their sources of financing; therefore, the best firms simply have more depth in relationships with willing lenders.

In fact, many commercial mortgage banking firms have direct and exclusive relationships with sources of financing for student housing deals that would be unavailable through other mortgage brokers. I speak from experience; if you have successfully closed a few deals and call several commercial mortgage brokers with good reputations explaining your desire to carry out large student housing transactions, the biggest and best mortgage brokers in town will immediately invite you out to lunch!

CONDUIT LOANS

As real estate investment property transactions have increased in size and sophistication, a public capital market that purchases large mortgages secured by real estate has been created. Investors looking for high-interest yields buy interests in pools of mortgages that have fixed rates and terms secured by commercial real estate. Large national banking organizations or commercial mortgage brokers generally put together these pools of mortgages. They originate the pools and sell off the group of property mortgages in the public capital markets.

These types of mortgage loans are called *conduits* because the originator acts as a conduit originating, packaging, and selling off a group of commercial mortgages for a profit. Investors are willing to pay a premium to the originator in exchange for an interest rate yield above the rates of bond alternatives of a similar length. Multifamily residential investment property loans make up the most desirable category of real estate for the public capital markets. As a result, loans for multifamily student housing become highly coveted mortgages for conduits.

Most Aggressive Loans

Without a doubt, conduits make up the most aggressive lenders in the marketplace today. While origination costs are high, interest rates on conduit loans can be significantly lower than the most attractive traditional bank financing. Plus, they have the advantage of no personal guarantee requirement.

Loan pricing is based on a premium or markup over the rate available at the time of the loan on the equivalent term Treasury bill. Low fixed rates for terms of up to ten years are common. Treasury bill yields are always low (compared with other bond investments) because of the perception of no-default risk. They prove to be a desirable benchmark from which to receive a mortgage interest rate quote.

For the obligation to be marketable in the public capital markets, conduit loans require fixed terms for a set period of time, with no right of prepayment. As an investor, that means you must be prepared to hold the property for the entire term of the loan, usually for up to ten years. (Note: The inability to prepay the balance often prevents an earlier sale.) It's never easy, but also it's not impossible to sell a property with a conduit loan before the end of the loan term.

Additionally, because the loan must withstand the capital market's scrutiny, expensive third-party reports and rigorous underwriting standards have become the norm. We are in the middle of putting together a conduit loan on a $4 million student housing acquisition as I write this chapter. This tough, complicated process requires daily attention answering information and document requests from the lender. We won't have our final interest rate locked in until the lender reaches a certain point in the commitment process. Still, my experience has taught me that on large deals that will be held for long periods, getting conduit loans is worth the extra cost and trouble. I know that, after this loan closes, I will look back at the process and realize that the pain was definitely worth bearing.

FANNIE MAE AS A LOAN RESOURCE

Although Fannie Mae is best known for creating mortgage products making home ownership possible for low- and moderate-income families, this organization leads in multifamily apartment building financing as well.

In addition to its traditional apartment building investment property products, Fannie Mae recently entered the student housing lending market with a Dedicated Student Housing Financing Program administered through 15 national commercial real estate mortgage brokerage firms. (The list of the participating firms and details of the Fannie Mae Student Housing Loan Program are available at *www.fanniemae.com.*)

If you have trouble finding an experienced commercial mortgage broker familiar within the student housing niche, turn to the list of the approved firms for Fannie Mae's Student Housing Loan Program for commercial mortgage brokers who are well connected to potential sources of financing.

Unlike other flexible loan products and sources, the Fannie Mae pilot Dedicated Student Housing Loan Program requires that owners provide no food service or other dormitory-type services. Maximum loan terms are 10 years with the amortization of principal repayments made over a 25-year repayment schedule.

Generally, interest rates on Fannie Mae loans are extremely attractive. Don't overlook this potential financing vehicle when you're seeking a mortgage for a qualifying student housing property.

Fannie Mae's Pilot Loan Program

To help meet the growing need for financing student housing, Fannie Mae's Dedicated Student Housing Loan Program offers unique features without recourse and no personal guarantees. It's specifically for apartment building purchases that cater to a student tenant base. Eligible properties must have undergraduate and graduate students making up at least 80 percent of the tenant base. Properties should be located close to a university that has at least 10,000 enrolled students. The properties must be within two miles of campus or on a university-sanctioned bus line.

OTHER FINANCING SOURCES

As student housing real estate has become more widely accepted as a quality property class, more lenders have entered the field and now actively seek transactions to finance. In today's competitive environment for loans on highly regarded investment real estate, investors are blessed with heavy competition from lenders for good quality deals. Specifically, good quality deals are properties located near campus or on a university-approved bus route at universities that have at least 10,000 full-time enrolled students.

A growing potential source of mortgage financing for student housing transactions is life insurance companies. Accessible through established commercial mortgage brokerage firms, life insurance companies are often excellent, low-cost providers of financing for commercial real estate transactions. Billions of dollars in life insurance company asset value is placed each year in commercial and investment property mortgages. Because the "word is out" on the demand for prime student housing properties, the number of life insurance companies seeking mortgage opportunities in the niche has grown.

THE EASY PART IS OVER

Have you found it difficult to acquire equity and leverage for your new student housing business? You'll find that after closing a deal or two, you'll change your mind. If you're a seasoned investor, you soon discover that the equity and debt components are the easiest parts of carrying on an investment real estate transaction. Far and away, the toughest component is finding properties worth buying, particularly in the student housing niche.

If you follow the equity raising and leveraging techniques and sources in this book, you won't miss—as long as you have identified a property worth buying. As you'll see in the next chapter, finding that prime property can be challenging, for it requires lots of time, effort, and knowledge.

FINDING STUDENT HOUSING PROPERTY WORTH BUYING

Once you have decided to enter the student housing investment real estate niche, the toughest part is finding a property worth buying. Even if it's easy to locate a piece of real estate available for sale near a major university campus, it can still be difficult determining if it provides the potential for a sufficient return and appreciation in value.

Be sure to cultivate lots of patience when it comes to real estate investing! It's impossible to know *when* the right deal will become available for purchase; it requires investigating ten or more deals to find one that's really worth owning. If you are too eager to enter the game and "pull the trigger" without conducting careful due diligence, you could become the owner of problem real estate. Remember, every opportunity needs to be investigated, lots of college campuses need to be researched, and dozens of buildings need to be inspected to make this work.

I suggest you proceed with caution. Student housing is an investment niche area in which the opportunity for cash flow and future price appreciation is so great that it will be well worth the wait for the right property. Patience is your greatest virtue when it comes to real estate investing.

GET THE WORD OUT

To start looking at student housing investment opportunities, put the word out that you want this particular asset class of real estate and "get in the game." The national real estate commercial brokerage firms become exclusive listing agents, at one time or another, for student housing properties placed on the market throughout the nation. Most national real estate brokerages have databases of potential buyers for all types of properties. And they provide e-mail notification systems for new listings. Therefore, to be a player in the student housing market, become a familiar face at the national commercial real estate brokerage companies. If you don't have a direct broker contact at the national firms already, start by perusing company Web sites to find contact information and join mailing lists.

A Very Local Business

Particularly in small college towns, the real estate business is a very local business. Local investors tend to own most of the assets in town. In addition, almost universally, two or three local real estate brokerage firms dominate the management and brokerage of student housing properties in most towns. Simply drive through any of these towns, note the management company signs on student housing properties, check out the Yellow Pages, and read the ads in the university student newspaper. You'll quickly determine who the dominant players are.

The easiest, most efficient way to start your search is to target a few college campuses in the high growth states (see Chapter 1) and "go back to school." There is no substitute for personally visiting the college town you've selected to get a feel for what's happening in that market.

Meet the Principals

After you have pinpointed the two or three dominate management companies, make an appointment to meet with one or more of the principals. When you introduce yourself, explain that you're looking for investment opportunities and want to be contacted if they have clients selling the kinds of properties you're looking for.

It's worthwhile to find out who owns the most desirable student housing properties in town. Also, make appointments to meet the principals of the building ownership firms. Let them know you are a qualified buyer looking to invest in that town's student housing market.

Don't be surprised at how many properties are *not* for sale. Honest, this is a good sign! Owners must know they have a good thing and can't replace their investment returns after selling their properties. But you will find, after a period of time, their thoughts may change because of estate planning, partner friction, or needs for liquidity. When an owner of a well-located student housing property wants to sell, you want to be positioned to receive the first call that person makes.

GET IN THE GAME

I have found that no matter how many real estate transactions I have completed or how much access I have to equity and financing, local college town owners and brokers allow me more credibility if I have successfully purchased properties of any size in their town. Properties could include a condo, town house, single-family house, even commercial space or multifamily housing. In fact, the first question sellers and local student housing brokers ask is, "Do you own any other properties near the local campus?" That tells me that carrying out the first deal in a targeted college market is critical to conducting business long-term in that market.

My advice about getting in the game is to first join a local apartment owners association. Establish local name recognition and gain access to the invaluable mailing list of other members. Then do a mailing to every campus student housing property owner introducing your firm. State that you're seeking confidential conversations about potential future acquisitions.

Your contacts often put introduction letters in a file, but could call you regarding an acquisition opportunity months or years later. At the same time, you're continuing to contact the national and local commercial real estate brokers to let them know you're interested in a particular college market. Make them aware that you've made an acquisition and want to expand your holdings.

In fact, the advantage of making your first buy in a targeted high enrollment growth college town is so great that, I must confess, I sometimes pay a bit more than I should or buy a less than superior location property. However, I never go crazy and put myself in a negative cash flow situation just for the sake of getting a toehold in a particular local market.

The Power of Momentum

I believe in the power of having momentum in the real estate business, especially in the student housing niche. A first deal leads to more investment opportunities and the potential to accumulate a large portfolio on a growing campus.

Disappointment Turned to Celebration

Our research indicated that the Illinois State University (ISU) campus in Normal, Illinois (our home state), was an ideal campus for a student housing investment. With its enrollment of 20,705 full-time students, the school was a well-respected public university in a high-growth population state. As the University of Illinois became tougher to get into, ISU became the school of choice for many of the state's growing college-age population and their parents seeking in-state public university tuition.

Representatives from one of the national real estate brokerage firms presented a one-year-old, well-located, 27-unit, 108-bed town house student housing property. Frankly, I was surprised that the property remained on the market for any length of time. I immediately got excited about the possibility of owning the complex. I was impressed with the marketing material and financial information furnished, but the asking price seemed too high. I assumed the owners were holding firm on the price, explaining that the building was not yet under contract.

The broker assured us the seller had room for negotiation in the price. He arranged for us to tour the property and meet with local owners. I was so worried about losing the deal to another buyer that I did some intelligence work in advance of our visit. I discovered that the owners had a relationship with one of the larger Chicago-area banks with whom we did business. I requested that the vice president in charge of lending at the bank—coincidentally, his daughter lived in the student housing complex—call the existing owners to assure them the bank would give us the money needed to close on the deal.

Based on our research that this property would fit our model, I wanted to make sure that, even in advance of our meeting and property tour, the current owners knew we legitimately had the financial ability to close on a transaction. The property turned out to be a high-quality asset and was physically extremely well built. The center of campus could be seen from the sidewalk in front of the property. Each bedroom was equipped with high-speed Internet access for which students paid an extra monthly fee. The all-brick structure featured large, 1,800-square-foot luxury town houses equipped with four bedrooms and four full baths, upgraded kitchen appliances, washers and dryers in the units, and individual central air and heating systems. All utilities were resident-paid; the only utility bill the owner paid for covered the lights in the parking lot.

While the property was listed for $5.5 million, our analysis of the probable actual first-year net operating income (NOI) indicated we could pay up to $4.8 million. We started the negotiations by offering $4.5 million, seeking a counteroffer, and hoping to end up at less than $4.8 million.

While we were negotiating, another buyer surfaced, offering $5.2 million. Even though the building was probably the nicest student housing property we've ever seen, we reluctantly followed our rules of discipline. We told the owners that we couldn't go above $4.8 million and that they should accept the $5.2 million offer.

Also based on our analysis and experience, I knew that the $5.2 million number just made no sense. I suspected the contract at that price would never close and asked the owners to contact us if things did not work out with the high bidder. I really felt badly about losing this one because the property was located on a campus we liked, was in great condition, and had an excellent location. Shortly after we lost the deal, we were presented with another acquisition opportunity on the ISU campus. Within a matter of two weeks, as many as six separate student housing properties were placed on the market and made available to us. On the one hand, we appreciated the opportunity to enter a campus market we had targeted by making multiple building purchases, but it seemed odd that so much was suddenly available for purchase. Something was going on at ISU that made us nervous and suspicious.

Investigating more deeply, we realized that the private student housing market had rapidly become overbuilt. An out-of-state firm was building a 122-unit, 475-bed brand-new student housing property close to campus. To get the property leased up for the coming fall term, the developer had been offering incentives as well as 10-month (rather than 12-month) leases. As a result, local student housing owners panicked and lowered rents. Consequently, there was negative rent growth in the student housing market at ISU.

To make matters worse, the university reiterated its policy of not allowing freshmen or sophomores to live outside of the university-owned dorms. What's more, freshmen enrollment actually decreased as the Board of Regents effectively capped admissions when it raised the minimum required ACT and high school grade-point average for acceptance.

As you might have already guessed, the owners of the town house deal had their broker call us within a couple of months of the original first bid for the property. Apparently, the higher bidder couldn't get the property to appraise for the valuation needed for a loan, and backed out of the contract during the due diligence period. The owners were now willing to take our offer of $4.8 million. When I balked based on the flood of properties available in the market, the broker pushed for an offer that might be accepted *below* the $4.8 million original price. Just a few months earlier, I'm sure we would have excitedly gone ahead with the acquisition at $4.8 million had our offer been accepted.

Hindsight is, of course, 20/20, but the owners and the unrealistic high bidder did us a favor. What seemed disappointing became a reason for celebration. Ironically, our mutual banking source—hungry to provide us with the financing—called to check on the status of the deal. Based on our continued monitoring of the Illinois State student housing market, we are seeing high vacancies, restricted enrollment, and private housing living policies, coupled with lower rents and higher vacancies for a few more years. Although we're always prepared to change our opinion based on new information, we are not interested in the ISU campus at this time, and have removed the school from our targeted potential markets of opportunity list.

If we end up overpaying on the first deal, we make it a small transaction and use our own money rather than take in outside investors. Why? Because to continue to raise money for future deals using outside investor money, I think it's important to maintain a high rate of return track record with syndicated outside-investor deals. Besides, we don't want to be responsible for investor money—or have to answer to others—on a deal that is less than a high return.

When attempting to find a property worth buying, I suggest you divide the items requiring investigation and due diligence into two categories: (1) factors external to the property and (2) items related to the targeted property itself. Both of these areas need to be fully investigated and evaluated to understand the viability of the investment.

FACTORS EXTERNAL TO THE TARGETED PROPERTY

Determining the future outlook for growth in enrollment at a particular college campus is fundamental when forecasting the growth in demand for private student housing. Often the enrollment plans for the university you're considering are available in a long-range-plan format, which you can access through the university Web site or from the Office of the University President. Obviously, a university with a policy encouraging growth in enrollment portends an excellent opportunity for high occupancy and increased rents near campus student housing rental properties.

The size and composition of the student body is also an important consideration. Universities with enrollments of fewer than 10,000 students generally don't have enough demand for privately owned student housing rental properties. The composition of the student body is also important because full-time students tend to require housing while part-time students are usually local residents who don't need independent housing. Many large universities, especially those located in or near large metropolitan areas, are commuter schools with a relatively small percentage of students living on or near campus.

Watch out. The statistics for commuter school enrollment numbers can be large and misleading, while the number of university-owned dorm rooms is usually low. The enrollment number—along with the university-owned-beds-to-enrolled-student ratio—can point to a positive student housing environment if they're viewed in a vacuum. Experience shows that commuter schools make for poor private student housing investments. As a result, unless a compelling reason exists, stay away from investing near universities located in major cities.

Quality and Type of Rooms Available

In addition to the number of beds owned by the university, it's worth exploring the age, quality, and type of university dorm rooms available. For example, it's tough to compete against new dorms with high-speed Internet access, individual kitchens and bathrooms, and central air-conditioning. Compare that with older, more obsolete, and amenity-sparse dorm rooms. For most students, living in university-owned dorms located near the center of campus is more desirable than living in far-off campus dorms that require a bus ride to get to classes.

Take time to learn your targeted university's student housing policies and understand their implications on a private student housing investment. For example, a university that requires freshmen *and* sophomores to live in university-owned dorms has set up a less favorable environment for private student housing owners than a school that allows all students to live in private housing.

Despite nationwide budget constraints plaguing state university systems, some institutions of higher learning are planning additions to the university-owned dorm room numbers through new construction programs. On the other side of the equation—and a more common circumstance that benefits private investors—many universities are closing obsolete dorms. So early on in your due diligence, find out about possible plans for replacing those rooms taken out of service.

New Construction of Student Housing Units

In your research, you'll find that privately owned new construction of student housing units has become fairly common on major college campuses. In fact, some college towns suffer from low occupancy levels because of overbuilding by the private sector. Some campus towns have actually seen foreclosures of new construction student housing development projects.

As new construction private housing units are added to the marketplace, the ratio of university-owned-beds-to-enrolled-students may remain attractive, but the number of available housing units in the market has still grown. Be sure to take a survey of new construction projects and planned developments before purchasing an existing student housing property on any college campus.

In addition, be aware that close-in available land sites portend the potential for new developments. If the site is large enough and market demand exists, you can count on the site being developed into student housing units. On the other side of the coin, a lack of available land sites close to campus creates a barrier to entry for new construction projects. This helps guarantee continued high occupancy levels for the existing student housing stock. Generally speaking, the more new construction going on in a particular college town, the more cautious you should be in acquiring only well-located, close-to-campus, new student housing properties.

Always be on the lookout for too much investment real estate in the student housing market. Even though it can cause frustration and test my ability to remain patient, I'm always more comfortable making an investment when the property was hard to come by. If I discover too many student housing property opportunities in a particular college market—especially for an extended length of time—I know trouble is brewing. If too many property owners all want to sell at the same time, that indicates they have difficulty finding renters and raising rents.

I recommend you perform the due diligence research work on factors external to the targeted property before you identify an actual acquisition possibility. While conducting this search, expect to wait a fair amount of time to get on top of these factors. The more you go through the process of researching a particular campus, the easier and quicker it will be when you check out the next university town. After a short while, you'll develop a gut feeling about the need for private student housing at any targeted university.

"Good News" Six Months Later

At one point, my partner and I were bullish about a particular college town market in the Midwest because of the college's growing enrollment and inadequate number of dorm rooms. We had located a close-in, new-construction, 160-bed town house development to buy, but we just couldn't get the sellers to come down to a reasonable (but fair) market price.

Six months after the initial negotiations broke down, the sellers' broker called with the "good news" that they were now willing to enter a contract at the price we were willing to pay. As it turned out, in the interim period, seven other student housing deals were actively being marketed for sale by other owners in the same market. The town was suffering from low occupancy and no rent growth because of a large near-campus apartment building that was offering special lease incentives for the first year. Despite the selling broker's excitement that we could get this deal at our offer price, we took a pass!

ITEMS RELATED TO THE TARGETED PROPERTY ITSELF

Once you've identified a potential acquisition property, the real work of crunching the numbers to underwrite the deal begins. Conduct some of that due diligence early on, completing the rest only after you've tied up the property at a negotiated price.

Letter of Intent

If you want to move forward with a transaction and take it to a more formal due diligence level, I suggest you tie up the price with a nonbinding Letter of Intent signed by the buyer and seller. (See a sample letter in Appendix B.) Do so in the early stages of the transaction. (If you're new to the real estate investment business, consult an attorney before drafting your Letter of Intent.)

Before we present a Letter of Intent on a property we might purchase, we do fairly comprehensive financial projections and, unless an unusual circumstance comes up, we make an on-site property inspection. Generally, the broker and/or owner reveal preliminary income and expense numbers and other data about the property. On a student housing property deal during this preliminary investigation stage, we also want to obtain (at a minimum) the current and future school year rent roll plus historical property operating expenses.

Net Operating Income

After reviewing seller-provided numbers combined with our own experience operating other investment properties, we then project a Property Operating Statement for the initial year and following years. Subtracting projected operating expenses from projected income gives us an estimated net operating income, known as the NOI. As we get further into the investigation, we make adjustments to the NOI based on new and better information. In my view, it's impossible to make an intelligent offer on a property without doing preliminary projections and calculating its projected net operating income.

In addition to rent, include potential income from these items: late charges, laundry, parking, vending machines, utility reimbursement, and damage deposit forfeiture revenue. Also calculate a reasonable amount of vacancy and collection loss based on the operating history of the property and other real estate investments in the community. Deduct that estimate from gross revenues to produce an effective gross income forecasted revenue number. Then deduct projected operating expenses from the effective gross income to derive the anticipated property net operating income.

Projected gross income − Projected operating expenses =
Net operating income

Operating Expenses

Typical operating expenses include real estate taxes, insurance, utilities (including cable and Internet connection charges), repairs and maintenance (including turnover costs), outside contracted services for lawn care, snow removal, cleaning; supplies, advertising, administrative expenses; fees for legal, accounting, and management services; and capital reserves and expenditures.

Once we estimate an NOI, if we still want to pursue buying a particular property given its asking price, we arrange for a tour to uncover unpleasant surprises. If we are satisfied with the potential for the building, we make our offer by submitting a Letter of Intent or, depending on the circumstances, submitting a binding contract as our initial offer. In all but a few exceptional situations, we reserve a reasonable contingency period of between 15 and 60 days to complete a full due diligence and feasibility study before our contract becomes binding.

Third-Party Investigative Reports

During the due diligence and feasibility period, we conduct extensive investigations to make sure our income and expense assumptions will hold up. We often order third-party investigative reports on the property. With a student housing investment opportunity, several important areas unique to the niche require confirmation during the due diligence period. For example, understanding the school year leasing cycle is crucial to predicting the income stream for the property. Clearly it's not relevant for other types of investment housing.

These reports may include environmental, engineering, mechanical systems, and roof evaluations, as well as independent valuation appraisals. Be sure to coordinate the entire feasibility study process so various experts can be brought through in a timely and logical manner. Have them complete all reports, verifications, and inspections before the contractually stated due diligence period ends. That way, you have an escape in case you discover items that negatively affect your original NOI projections.

Lease Sign-ups

Unlike traditional residential investment property leases with varying terms and expiration dates, student housing residential leases tend to begin and end on the same day. Just imagine the impact that creates for managing a building! If nothing has been done to renew or release apartments with leases that expire on the same day, all at once the income on the property goes down to absolutely zero! What's more, if the timing on the leasing cycle season is off, the apartment units could remain empty for an entire year.

Student housing properties at most major universities commonly require students to enter into 12-month leases that begin either in August (at the beginning of the fall term) or in May (at the end of the previous school year). It's essential to know the local lease cycle for the targeted property—along with the progress being made toward lease sign-up—so you can anticipate the income stream over the next year.

For example, if a building goes on the market in July and the lease cycle for the college town begins in May, find out how much of it is already leased. At that point, you can project any unoccupied apartments remaining vacant until the following May. If the apartments aren't rented by the time the majority of students go home for the summer, you'll have a tough time filling the empty units for the fall. Sure, there may be an influx of new students seeking apartments for the spring term starting in January, but the numbers will be small compared to the fall lease-up period.

Additional Review Items

While in the due diligence contingency period on a deal, we verify our income and expense numbers by checking the existence of all written leases covering the term and rental rates projected. We review copies of paid bills and property tax returns and closely inspect the building's physical condition. We also review the property for any urgently needed capital improvements, deferred maintenance issues, and appearance upgrades. Because students have become a demanding housing consumer group, we realize properties need to be well maintained and upgraded to stay full and sustain rental rate increases from year to year.

What Students Require!

To be specific, student housing rental units today require high-speed Internet access, laundry facilities on-site or in the apartment, and full kitchens and modern bathrooms. Furnished units commonly provide central air-conditioning, balconies, dishwashers, and microwave ovens. If a property under review lacks these important features and competitive properties offer them, it would be wise to budget in the cost of upgrading to include them. In addition, the availability of on-site parking is fast becoming a necessity.

Price Adjustments

If the due diligence and feasibility reviews turn up bad news that would have a *small* impact on NOI projections or required capital investment, I usually let the transaction close anyway. Although one school of thought says, "Play it tough and fight for every dollar to get purchase price adjustments," I find that it's usually not worth the hassle to insist on that. After all, brokers, sellers, and lawyers involved in one transaction usually show up when you're conducting transactions in the future. If you become perceived as a tough buyer looking for the last buck, your offer could be avoided in favor of one from more cooperative buyers. I would much rather be perceived as the nice guy (or patsy), especially when doing so costs me little money and positions me to get the first call on the next deal.

However, when your due diligence reveals major problems that will have a *large* impact on NOI or increased capital improvement requirements, you can either walk away from the deal or seek a purchase price concession to stay committed to it. If the adjustment required because of undiscovered or undisclosed issues is too high, it's best to tell the seller you're withdrawing from the contract "pursuant to a feasibility inspection contingency clause" rather than seek a substantial price reduction. In my experience, if the problems you uncover are so great, you're dealing with a dishonest seller who wants to hide problems with the property. It means you'll likely face even more hidden problems in the future.

As a third possibility, if the issues are relatively minor (rather than problems intentionally covered up) and if the deal can still work with a relatively minor price reduction, stay committed to closing in exchange for receiving a price concession. Provided with a documentation of problems, reasonable sellers and brokers usually cooperate to work out a price reduction rather than remarket the property. If they hold firm to their price, you have a decision to make: does the deal still make sense to you?

Final Setup Requirements

During this phase, also line up final mortgage financing, put out feelers to raise equity if needed, and check and recheck all your investigations and inspections. If you become uncomfortable with the assumptions used in your projections—the quality of the building, the property's location, the college town student housing market, or any aspect that worries you—reevaluate the deal *now* and possibly get out of it. Remember, once the contingency period runs out, the contract becomes binding and you'll be legally obligated to close, putting your earnest money at risk for forfeiture.

IDEAL ATTRIBUTES

The ideal student housing property worth buying includes these attributes:

- New property possesses modern amenities.
- Located on or near a major public university campus (within walking distance).

- Located in a high enrollment growth state that has a low university-owned-dorm-beds-to-enrolled-students ratio.
- Community has old, obsolete university-owned dorm rooms.
- University has an unrestricted policy allowing *all* students to live in private housing.
- No competition exists from new-construction student housing.
- Growing enrolled student body population has at least 10,000 full-time students.

In the real world, not every property worth buying will fit this ideal. Most will lack one or more of these ideal attributes. In fact, properties that meet every one of the ideal attributes often attract multiple offers and sell to overzealous and optimistic buyers willing to overpay. Therefore, never forget the discipline required to walk away from a deal that's overpriced and doesn't provide enough cash flow to cover expenses, contingency reserves, mortgage payments, and a reasonable return on the equity investment.

When Not All Factors Exist

If some of these ideal property attributes are missing, I've found that "location near the center of campus" trumps all other problems. Obviously, the ideal location alone can't turn a dilapidated slum in need of substantial repair into a desirable high-occupancy building (although, on many campuses, location can overcome these problems as well). However, on most campuses in high-growth states with favorable university-owned-beds-to-student ratios, a location that's a block or two from the quad frequently yields 100 percent occupancy and yearly rent increases.

The rule of thumb is that the more negative issues with a campus or a building, the more important the property location becomes. Properties located in close proximity to campus lease up ahead of (and for more money than) locations farther out.

Location Always Wins Out

On every college campus I have ever looked at, I've found that for every negative attribute or less-than-ideal feature, a better location can compensate. For inferior farther-out locations, make sure that every other ideal student housing property attribute is present.

Next, let's look specifically at the types of investment transactions available to the student housing investor in Part Three.

STUDENT HOUSING TRANSACTIONS

Take a ride to any large campus college town and you will see many types of campus-related rental units. There are lots of ways to acquire and grow a portfolio in the student housing investment property business. A novice might want to start small, but a more experienced or highly capitalized investor might want to jump in and buy a large, intensive student housing investment.

The chapters in Part Three examine university-driven housing investment opportunities based on the following property types:

- Single-family homes and condominiums
- Multifamily residential apartment buildings
- Privately owned dorms and public-private partnerships
- Condominium developments near campus

After reviewing various potential student housing property types, we examine in detail the risks and dangers inherent in all student housing property niche acquisitions. Part Three concludes with a recap of the recent discovery of the student housing real estate arena by institutional investors and the public markets including the New York Stock Exchange.

6

INVESTING IN SINGLE-FAMILY HOMES AND CONDOMINIUMS

The easiest and lowest-cost way to enter the student housing business is to purchase a detached single-family home or a condominium in a college town and rent it to students. Finding the best house or condominium to buy is actually the hardest part. Ideally, you've already identified a campus with a growing student enrollment with a low university-owned-beds-to-student ratio.

SINGLE-FAMILY HOMES

Detached single-family homes in close proximity to campus have been traditional and desirable places for students to rent while attending college. In most (but certainly not all) college towns, the detached single-family home stock consists of older, vintage-style homes. Along with the institutions of higher learning themselves, college town single-family homes were often built nearly 100 years ago. While many homes have been rehabbed and renovated over the years, vintage properties as residential real estate rentals still provide unique challenges and issues.

Property Condition

When purchasing an older single-family home as a student housing rental investment, it's imperative that you complete a thorough inspection of all mechanical and structural systems of the home. Although you can find a single-family home investment property near a popular college campus for as little as $100,000, the property may need extensive repairs and capital improvements. The costs to replace the roof and the heating, electrical, and plumbing systems can together easily exceed the cost of the real estate itself. Although rental income and operating expenses are easy enough to verify, when it comes to investing in a single-family home as a rental property, the economics of the deal turn on the property condition and the need for capital improvements, now or in the near future.

Finding a well-qualified, independent property inspector is crucial to understanding the investment, especially for older properties that might have deferred maintenance issues. Although the trend is changing in most states, home inspectors are unlicensed and have no education or experience requirements. My own unwritten rule is to never accept the selling real estate broker's recommendation when it comes to home inspectors. Too many home inspectors and real estate agents have cozy referral arrangements that make me, as a buyer, nervous. Although there are certainly exceptions, home inspectors referred by a selling real estate agent are unlikely to kill a deal with a poor report.

I recommend you find a highly respected home inspector or a general contractor familiar with single-family home construction and mechanical systems where you live. Then pay for his or her transportation to do an on-site inspection in a remote city. It's worth the cost. Until you've established yourself in the targeted college town and built relationships with local vendors, it's difficult to judge their competence. Unless you have a local, independent, experienced contact in the college town you can trust for recommendations, pay the extra cost to import your own talent when it comes to home inspections.

Local Ordinance Considerations

This recent trend negatively impacts investments in single-family homes for rental to students: Towns, in increasing numbers, have legislated away the big house rental to a large number of students. In an effort to eliminate the classic obnoxious college parties and *Animal House* antics, permanent neighborhood residents have put pressure on local city halls to legislate out the classic four-bedroom, five-bedroom, or six-bedroom home rented out to a group of six or more party-loving, impermanent students. No one wants to live next door to a large house rented to undergraduates living away from home without parental supervision. In response, many college town communities have passed laws preventing more than three or four unrelated people from occupying the same dwelling unit.

What once were guaranteed, high-occupancy, student housing money machines have become large, old, empty houses on many college campuses. Be careful and check the local ordinances. Find out about any current community pressure before you buy that "perfect" charming, large, old house within walking distance to the center of campus, expecting to fill it with student renters.

CONDOMINIUMS

I like condominiums as an entry-level investment in the student housing rental market niche, but I have a bias toward them. As a part of my own real estate investment business aside from the student housing niche, I develop and convert apartment buildings into condominiums for sale to the public. My own bias aside, they're great entry-level investments because they're easy to understand in terms of operating costs and valuation.

Unlike detached single-family homes in which all costs are absorbed by the owner, the operating costs of a condominium are shared. The ongoing operating expenses of a condominium building are administered by members of the property's condominium association and the costs for maintenance of the common elements of the building are covered in the monthly assessment paid to the association. Unless there's a maintenance issue with a mechanical system or appliance in the condominium unit itself, the cost of repairs should be covered by the condominium association.

Although exceptions always exist, condominium buildings in close proximity to college campuses are relatively new phenomena, so they're often newer in construction with little deferred maintenance or capital improvement needs. Additionally, most condominiums are two or three bedrooms and accommodate a small enough number of student renters to fall below any local ordinance prohibitions.

Another advantage of condominiums is that the market value and potential resale valuation are easier to predict than individual, freestanding homes. Because they have similar units and layouts in the same building with a market and resale history, it's possible to track comparable sales and market valuation trends for condominiums more efficiently and with better data than for detached, single-family home sales. In most markets, well-located condominiums in desirable buildings sell faster than detached single-family homes. This creates a more liquid asset should you have a need or desire to sell the investment.

DON'T FORGET THE FUNDAMENTALS

Just because detached, single-family homes and condominiums are for sale on college campuses and have a relatively low investment requirement to "get in the game," it doesn't mean you can ignore investment property fundamentals. On the contrary, *because* of these low barriers to entry in this type of property investment, you need to be especially careful. Only pull the trigger if you're comfortable with the property's current and future cash flow as well as the potential for appreciation. Remember, you're often competing with owner/occupiers who tend to view the purchase price as an investment in a place to live and don't require a return on their investment.

Homebuyers want a nice place to live and most often stretch on price as far as they can afford for the largest and nicest home possible. Their decision more likely turns on the answer to the question: What can I afford based on my income? In contrast, your investment decision must turn on the answer to the questions:

- What is the net operating income?
- Is there positive cash flow after my debt service?
- Will there be appreciation in value over time?

When there's too much interest in the property from potential owner/occupiers, residential real estate investment opportunities usually don't make sense. Successful real estate investors run the numbers and exercise patience. If you look at enough deals and stay with it, you'll find the ones that make sense. Be prepared. Most detached, single-family homes and condominiums won't make good investment sense when you do the analysis. But some will, so be ready to go for it when you find them!

BUYING FOR YOUR CHILD'S USE

Many entrepreneurial parents of college students begin to explore purchasing a single-family home or condominium for their sons or daughters to occupy once they learn the cost to rent housing on a major college campus. They see the rental payments going out to a third-party landlord, and with investor instincts, they envision saving rent and getting a return on investment by buying and owning their own college town real estate. This instinct and logic points in the right direction, but often misses an important component of the investment decision. Let me explain.

I own a student housing apartment building on the campus of the same college where my daughter is enrolled. She doesn't live in the building and I pay full, fair-market rent for her to a total stranger in another building. No, I haven't lost my mind nor am I throwing away money. Here's the reason: By letting your own kid live there for no rent, you're giving up the opportunity to rent the unit to another student at full, fair-market value. Stated another way, the missed opportunity cost of a student housing rental occupied by your child is equal to the fair-market rent you're not receiving. Don't deceive yourself—in this business there's really no such thing as free rent!

Recognizing the missed opportunity cost of providing a rent-free location for your child, you may still decide to purchase a home or condo because of the potential for appreciation and the ability to derive some tax benefits. Before you do, here's one more factor to consider: More often than not, your child will have a roommate. The roommate is usually one of your son's or daughter's best friends and will still be required to pay rent.

Despite the friendship involved, and especially because of it, I strongly recommend a formal written lease for roommates occupying a home or condo you own, as well as guarantees from the roommate's parents. Your investment was made as an alternative to paying out rent for your child and to make money in the process. The investment needs to be treated as a business. Therefore, the roommate and his or her parents need to understand that all of the obligations under the lease agreement must be met. If the roommate is looking for free rent or latitude on making late rental payments, tell the parents to buy their own place rather than take advantage of you!

If the investment makes sense, complete the deal and rent out the property to any third parties in arm's-length transactions. You don't save money by not paying yourself rent for your own child, plus the lost opportunity cost of the missing rental value is too great. The investment needs to stand on its own. If you're only buying a place for your kid to live in for four years and not to maximize your investment opportunity, don't bother. Instead, pay out the rent and buy something else, perhaps on another campus.

The Ups and Downs of College Towns

Never forget that college towns are, for the most part, small towns. If you are an out-of-town real estate investor entering the market in a particular college town and aren't used to conducting business in small towns, always remember that you're *not* a part of the small town community but you're doing business in an environment different than you're accustomed to. I have learned that the business community—and particularly the real estate business community—in small college towns is very small.

Members of the local real estate community all know each other well, see each other around town, and probably even grew up together. The same players are involved over and over again in multiple numbers of real estate transactions; everyone knows the local real estate lawyers, bankers, title companies, and brokers. For that matter, everyone in the local business community knows everyone else in town!

I like doing business in college towns partly because it's different than doing business in Chicago, my hometown. College town businesspeople and professionals tend to be less hurried, much friendlier, very honest, and unusually helpful.

On the other hand, beware. There are no secrets within the small-town business community, which is a handicap when you want to keep real estate transactions secret. If a potential transaction is still in the confidential stage, don't make the mistake of calling the town's city hall, as I once did, to check on zoning and outstanding building code violations. You won't be talking to a nameless clerk. Instead, you're talking to a local public servant, who is probably friends with several potential competing buyers and real estate brokers. In fact, I had to face an aggressive local competing buyer within a day of my "friendly" conversation with a representative in the town's building department.

Don't meet with local management companies until the property is under contract and tied up. The word will be on the street soon enough; you don't want to fan the fire until you're sure that the property is under a binding contract and can't be sold to a local buyer who gets tipped off to the potential transaction. The local assessor will probably know the purchase price for the property before you close and the local lending sources will find out your finance source and the interest rate you paid for your loan.

No one means any harm and most businesspeople in the community are more than willing to do business with you. It's simply what happens when carrying on a real estate transaction as an outsider in a small town. You just need to be aware of the situation. I was once really freaked out and comforted at the same time when I made a reservation at a hotel in a college town and phoned ahead to reserve the hotel conference room for due diligence meetings. The desk clerk informed me that the conference room had already been reserved by a local real estate broker who helpfully coordinated meetings for me so I could complete my inspections of the apartment property I was buying. Amazing. The hotel clerk at the local Hilton knew who I was, why I was checking into the hotel, and who I was meeting with when I called to make the reservation. Talk about customer service!

7

MULTIFAMILY RESIDENTIAL APARTMENT BUILDINGS

If you're serious about the real estate investment business and want to enter the student housing niche, start by purchasing apartment buildings serving major university campuses. This is "where the action is" in the student housing business.

If you don't have the personal finances or money-raising ability to buy a campus apartment building as an initial investment, start small and aspire to move up to multifamily apartment building transactions. And if you only plan to purchase a house or condominium or two, you've made a passive investment that should provide an excellent supplement to your other sources of income and wealth generation.

If, however, you've decided to devote your primary business career to real estate investing, you can't afford to miss the opportunity to get into student housing. You can stake a significant claim to a piece of the student housing market by purchasing an apartment building—and eventually multiple apartment buildings—on major university campuses.

MAKING MONEY THE OLD-FASHIONED WAY

My early childhood memories include visions of walking through apartment buildings and conducting property inspections with my dad. Although I'm disciplined enough to do thorough investigations and complete comprehensive due diligence before every apartment building acquisition (I have partners and lenders I feel responsible to), I can usually tell at the initial showing if the deal will work.

Unlike any other business I'm aware of, investing in apartment building properties—either traditional or student housing—provides a proven method to use other people's money to produce income for now and build wealth for the future. By purchasing an apartment building using a mortgage lender's money for 80 percent of the purchase price (as is common in the residential income-producing apartment property business), the investor has used the lending institution's money to take ownership and control of a real estate asset. While the investor (or partnership group) has used only 20 percent of his or her own money for the purchase, he or she owns 100 percent of the property and is entitled to 100 percent of the building cash flow after the payment of the monthly mortgage amount.

In a situation even more unique to the real estate investment business, the property owner can choose to pay off the mortgage loan balance using other people's money. The mortgage principal balance, as well as the interest and other expenses of the property, can be paid off by using the rent payments made to the building owner by the property tenants. Over the life of the mortgage, the rent-paying students provide the funds to pay off the 80 percent loan obtained to purchase the investment.

When the apartment building is sold or refinanced, the only amount due to the original mortgage lender is the unpaid balance of the mortgage, not the full original 80 percent of the purchase price received from the lender. That's because of equity

How to Become a Millionaire

It's possible to become a multimillionaire by acquiring enough properties with sufficient cash flow to pay off mortgages and reap the benefits of equity buildup. As a simple illustration, take a $1 million property, acquired with an $800,000 mortgage and $200,000 of investor equity. Let's say the mortgage is set up to fully amortize, or pay off, in 20 years, and the property produces an annual cash flow sufficient to make the mortgage payments. In 20 years, the building will be owned free and clear.

Remember, the debt has been paid off, in full, by using other people's money because the student apartment renters have provided the income stream to retire the debt. If the building was properly underwritten and the due diligence techniques described in this book were used before acquiring it, the investor will own a property valued at $1 million, free and clear, while having invested only $200,000. The investor became a millionaire on this one single apartment building investment, assuming the building has not depreciated in value one cent.

buildup, which is defined as the amount by which the mortgage principal has been paid down. I love the concept of equity buildup; the savvy real estate investor earns equity buildup and accumulates net worth *even if the property doesn't appreciate in value.*

Added Punch of Almost Certain Appreciation in Value

The real beauty of investing in student housing apartment buildings today is their near-guaranteed appreciation. Based on undeniable demographic trends—namely the coming of the echo boomer generation to college—well-located student housing apartment buildings on major university campuses will increase in value over the next several years. There's not much in life, or investing, that's certain, but with an unstoppable explosion in the number of students seeking student housing over the next 20 years, it's safe to count on housing shortages and resulting rent increases. As rents increase, so will cash flow and NOI. I've tried to hold back my enthusiasm throughout this book by pointing out possible pitfalls, but I can't hold back my excitement. Why? Because I can predict with near certainty major appreciation in student housing real estate assets over the next two decades.

It's time to take off my Mr. Conservative caution hat when it comes to the prospects for appreciation of multifamily apartment buildings in general and well-located student housing apartment buildings on high-growth campuses in particular. The fact of the matter is, investors who buy student housing apartment buildings will see much greater increases in their net worth than what old-fashioned equity buildup can provide alone. That $1 million student housing apartment building purchased today will increase the investor's net worth by far more than the equity buildup.

Okay, we won't know just how right I am for 20 years, but based on the trends I see, the investor of a $1 million building is going to be more than a millionaire in 20 years. He or she will most assuredly become a multimillionaire on just one apartment building investment. Leverage the effect of the combination of equity buildup and appreciation in value over multiple apartment properties at one or more universities. We're talking serious money!

The Deal We Thought We'd Lost

Purdue University in West Lafayette, Indiana, has a rich history and famous alumni including Neil Armstrong, the first man to walk on the moon. With more than 38,000 enrolled full-time students and 11,525 university-owned beds, the school has a favorable 29.81 percent university-owned-beds-to-enrolled-students ratio. Purdue is the only Big Ten University to allow freshmen to live outside of the dorms. As a result, close-in student housing properties consistently attain 100 percent occupancy levels.

We learned of an extremely well-located and rarely available fully occupied student housing property consisting of 39 units and 152 beds on the market. We immediately made an appointment for a property tour. But between the time we contacted the listing broker to see the property and our appointment less than a week later, it went under contract to an investment group from California. I was disappointed when the broker called to cancel our appointment without giving us the opportunity to submit an offer. The California group had submitted a full-price offer that was too tempting for the owners to delay.

I gave the broker my standard "We are here if things don't work out" speech and stressed our ability to close the transaction quickly without the need for a mortgage contingency because we already had our financing lined up. Given the great location, the cash flow of the property, and the reasonableness of the asking price, I didn't expect to hear again from the broker. I chalked this one up in the one-more-lost-opportunity column.

Three weeks later, I received a call from the broker indicating the property was back on the market and available to us for a quick close at a discount of $150,000 off the $4,150,000 listing price. Apparently, the California group was trading out of another property and had identified three potential acquisitions, including the Purdue property. This group had tied up all three deals for 21 days subject to an inspection. Having never purchased a student housing property before, they didn't understand the deal and selected a traditional apartment building property in Denver instead. The buyers sent notice to the Purdue property owners backing out of the contract on the last day of the due diligence inspection period. The owners of the Purdue property were breaking up their partnership and, having a taste of being under contract, wanted a real deal that would close. It was time to move rapidly and pull the trigger!

I reassured the broker that we were serious players and wanted to buy the property. We arrived on the Purdue campus and took a property tour within a few days of the phone call. The building met our expectations, had been maintained well, and had a well-documented 100 percent occupancy history. Everything we saw looked good—including the pleasant surprise that some of the rents at the property were currently under market. That created the opportunity to enhance our income by raising rents in the fall.

We tied up the property sale and went right to contract. Although minor problems surfaced in the due diligence phase, everything checked out well in the end. As this book is being written, we're under contract to close on this Purdue property and feel excited about the potential for future enhanced cash flow and appreciation in value. We're carrying out this deal with our joint venture partner, plus we're in the process of raising equity through syndication. Our 80 percent, nonrecourse mortgage financing has been arranged through a commercial mortgage broker with a major life insurance company.

In this business, you just never know when a deal you thought you'd lost comes back to you. Often, transactions don't close for a variety of reasons. Always keep the door open and never burn bridges with sellers or brokers. Create an environment in which everyone feels comfortable calling you back when another deal doesn't work out. Set the tone with people you deal with so they'll be at ease when contacting you again about a deal gone bad.

Clearly, patience and perseverance are great virtues in the real estate investment business.

MULTIFAMILY AND MIXED-USE PROPERTIES

The most common form of housing for students living in college towns, outside of the university-owned dorms, is privately owned, multifamily apartment buildings. Major university campuses tend to have a number of apartment buildings near campus. Occupancy levels at the best campuses for investment run as high as 95 percent to 100 percent. The types of apartment buildings near campuses vary from vintage properties to new construction luxury apartment complexes.

Additionally, campus student housing options increasingly include apartment options in mixed-use buildings. Typically located on major commercial streets in campus towns, these buildings have retail tenants on the street level and student rental apartments on the upper floors. As retailers and service businesses expand on college campuses, the mixed-use student housing category will grow. Particularly when they have major national retailers as lower-level long-term storefront tenants, mixed-use student housing properties provide an excellent and secure investment opportunity.

As universities' enrollments increase and campuses expand, the universities themselves often need additional office space for departments and programs. Most major universities have outgrown their school-owned office buildings and rent office space from private landlords with near-campus locations. University office space leases provide stable and creditworthy income streams for building owners. As university office space needs expand because of unprecedented growth, look for more opportunities for mixed-use student housing properties at major universities.

REHAB AND REPOSITION OPPORTUNITIES

A niche within a niche is emerging as students demand more amenities and luxury conveniences in their housing apartments.

Within this niche exists the opportunity to take old, rundown apartment buildings, then rehab and reposition them to achieve greater rents and boost property values. This trend echoes the renaissance taking place in most American urban centers with the rehab and modernization of vintage rental properties.

Investors desiring an active development role will find opportunities at most major universities to rehab out-of-date buildings into modern, amenity-filled—translated, higher-rent—apartment complexes. Depending on the condition of the property and the potential for return on investment, options in this area start with cosmetic rehab of kitchens and baths and new carpet to full-gut rehabs with all new mechanical systems and floor plans. This is not an area for the uninitiated or inexperienced, but if you've successfully completed rehabs of traditional apartments, you might want to explore rehab opportunities on college campuses.

Based on my experience in both the student housing niche and the rehab and repositioning of apartment buildings in the Chicago area, I sense that most markets are ripe for student housing rehab projects. If you can buy an "old beater" apartment building at the right price, rehabbing it would add tremendous value. The increased rents that result would immediately contribute to its appreciation.

NEW-CONSTRUCTION OPPORTUNITIES

Investors with ground-up building and development experience and an appetite for active involvement in a university town should also look for opportunities to build new apartment buildings for student occupancy. It stands to reason that as enrollments increase and demand for private apartment rentals continues to grow, today's rental housing stock will be inadequate for tomorrow's student population.

New-construction development can be a risky part of the real estate investment business. Only attempt it with experienced builders and developers, particularly in remote college town locations. In fact, I feel that new-construction student housing development is so specialized and risky that I don't recommend it to the average student housing real estate investor. Even for the more experienced new-construction developer investors, I caution you to only consider a new-construction student housing apartment project with an experienced and trustworthy local college town joint venture partner. You could lose your shirt fast!

CAMPUS APARTMENT CHARACTERISTICS

In a September 2004 survey of 64 major university student housing markets, the National Multi Housing Council (NMHC) compiled data on the state of student housing property characteristics in privately owned campus apartment buildings. Property characteristics varied widely from campus to campus.

Property Age

The NMHC survey confirms that a great deal of the nation's student housing stock is getting old. Most private student housing apartment properties were built in the 1970s and 1980s to accommodate the last large enrollment increases of the baby boom generation. The University of Dayton in Ohio has the oldest student housing stock in the survey with its average apartment property built in 1961.

At the other end of the spectrum, Georgia Southern University has the newest student housing apartment stock with the average year built pegged at 1996. Three other schools with modern, average-age student housing properties include Auburn University in Alabama, with an average apartment property build date of 1993; the University of Central Arkansas, 1992; and the University of Georgia, 1990.

University campuses with aging housing stock provide the best opportunities for rehab and modernization of apartment buildings—and charging increased rents. The oldest student housing apartment stock, based on the average year built, was found at the following schools, according to the NMHC survey:

Oldest Student Housing Apartment Building Stock by Average Year Built

University of Dayton	1961
University of Minnesota	1964
University of Michigan	1964
Old Dominion University (VA)	1964
Syracuse University (NY)	1965
Idaho State University	1966
University of Maryland–College Park	1967
University of Connecticut	1968
Stanford University (CA)	1970
University of Wisconsin	1971

In contrast, the campus with the newest student housing stock according to the survey follows:

Newest Student Housing Apartment Building Stock by Average Year Built

Georgia Southern University	1996
Auburn University (AL)	1993
University of Central Arkansas	1992
University of Georgia	1990
Illinois State University	1989
University of California–Irvine	1988
University of Texas–Austin	1988
Clemson University (SC)	1987
University of Arkansas–Fayetteville	1987
Appalachian State University	1986

University private housing stocks with newer average-age construction dates tend to indicate campuses with recent, private, student housing apartment property under new construction. While the campus may still have aging, obsolete properties as well, the average age usually comes down as a result of a recent construction boom adding a large number of units in the campus town.

You should exercise caution before entering the market with an acquisition if the average age of private student housing stock is becoming newer. Where average building age is new, check and recheck the environment during the due diligence stage. You want to make sure there hasn't been overbuilding of private apartment buildings serving the campus.

Remember, when you have a campus with newer average-age housing stock, stay closer to the center of campus and buy newer construction, high-amenity properties. Be especially careful of farther-out, old properties in a college town with a new average housing stock age. Conversely, there may be a significant opportunity for acquiring an older property in the right location on a campus with a newer average building age. A close-in, well-located aging property on a campus with much newer construction farther out from the center of campus could provide an excellent high-occupancy rehab and repositioning opportunity for active investors.

Average Rents

As with traditional multifamily investment properties, the NMHC study found that average rents for student housing apartment properties vary widely from region to region, and within regions in individual campus town communities. It will come as no surprise to experienced real estate investors that California universities survey as having the highest average rents in the nation for most student housing apartment rental options. Generally, the types of apartment rentals available at most universities include studio, one-bedroom, two-bedroom, three-bedroom, and the increasingly popular four-bedroom rental option.

Among the 64 university markets surveyed, the NMHC study indicated the following highest average monthly rent college campuses:

Highest Average Monthly Rent

Unit Type	University	Average Monthly Rent
Studio	University of California–Irvine	$1,270
Studio	Stanford University (CA)	975
Studio	San Jose University (CA)	877
Studio	Cornell University (NY)	800
Studio	Rutgers University (NJ)	775
1-Bedroom	University of California–Irvine	1,302
1-Bedroom	Stanford University (CA)	1,287
1-Bedroom	San Jose University (CA)	1,041
1-Bedroom	Cornell University (NY)	1,039
1-Bedroom	Rutgers University (NJ)	1,013
2-Bed/1-Bath	Stanford University (CA)	1,535
2-Bed/1-Bath	University of California–Irvine	1,465
2-Bed/1-Bath	San Jose University (CA)	1,272
2-Bed/1-Bath	Rutgers University (NJ)	1,187
2-Bed/1-Bath	Cornell University (NY)	1,169
2-Bed/2-Bath	Stanford University (CA)	1,919
2-Bed/2-Bath	Rutgers University (NJ)	1,666
2-Bed/2-Bath	University of California–Irvine	1,601
2-Bed/2-Bath	San Jose State University (CA)	1,444
2-Bed/2-Bath	University of Maryland–College Park	1,417
3-Bed/2-Bath	Stanford University (CA)	2,271
3-Bed/2-Bath	University of California–Irvine	1,978

3-Bed/2-Bath	San Jose State University (CA)	1,844
3-Bed/2-Bath	University of Wisconsin	1,584
3-Bed/2-Bath	Cornell University (NY)	1,533
3-Bed/3-Bath	San Jose State University (CA)	2,150
3-Bed/3-Bath	University of Texas	1,955
3-Bed/3-Bath	University of Colorado	1,700
3-Bed/3-Bath	Indiana University	1,590
3-Bed/3-Bath	University of Virginia	1,456
4-Bed/2-Bath	Cornell University (NY)	2,375
4-Bed/2-Bath	University of Virginia	2,130
4-Bed/2-Bath	Penn State University	1,983
4-Bed/2-Bath	University of Wisconsin	1,828
4-Bed/2-Bath	University of Iowa	1,467

According to the NMHC survey, the lowest average monthly rents, with some notable exceptions, are concentrated in the southern states:

Lowest Average Monthly Rent

Unit Type	University	Average Monthly Rent
Studio	Clemson University (SC)	$250
Studio	Auburn University (AL)	285
Studio	University of Alabama	307
Studio	Idaho State University	310
Studio	New Mexico State University	320
1-Bed/1-Bath	Idaho State University	321
1-Bed/1-Bath	University of Central Arkansas	369
1-Bed/1-Bath	Auburn University (AL)	377
1-Bed/1-Bath	Clemson University (SC)	392
1-Bed/1-Bath	Oklahoma State University	397

2-Bed/1-Bath	University of Central Arkansas	417
2-Bed/1-Bath	Georgia Southern University	425
2-Bed/1-Bath	Idaho State University	438
2-Bed/1-Bath	Oklahoma State University	460
2-Bed/1-Bath	University of Missouri	466
2-Bed/2-Bath	Georgia Southern University	500
2-Bed/2-Bath	Oklahoma State University	540
2-Bed/2-Bath	University of Central Arkansas	552
2-Bed/2-Bath	University of Arkansas–Fayetteville	587
2-Bed/2-Bath	New Mexico State University	588
3-Bed/2-Bath	Georgia Southern University	550
3-Bed/2-Bath	Old Dominion University (VA)	551
3-Bed/2-Bath	Clemson University (SC)	552
3-Bed/2-Bath	University of Arkansas–Fayetteville	576
3-Bed/2-Bath	Bowling Green State University (OH)	630
3-Bed/3-Bath	University of South Carolina	685
3-Bed/3-Bath	Auburn University (AL)	865
3-Bed/3-Bath	University of Kentucky	895
3-Bed/3-Bath	Purdue University (IN)	900
3-Bed/3-Bath	East Carolina University	995
4-Bed/2-Bath	University of Oklahoma	400
4-Bed/2-Bath	Georgia Southern University	699
4-Bed/2-Bath	University of Dayton (OH)	825
4-Bed/2-Bath	Kansas State University	1,001
4-Bed/2-Bath	University of Kansas	1,089

Property Amenities

The desires and expectations of today's student renter to have amenities can't be overstated and warrants repetition. The echo boom generation expects far more luxury in student housing living than previous generations did. The days of renting any property near campus, in any condition, and accepting unreturned phone calls to the local landlord for service and repairs are definitely over. Student renters of today are sophisticated and demanding consumers requiring the finest in amenities and responsive customer service from property owners and management companies.

Typical property amenities prevalent in the student housing marketplace include fitness centers, study lounges, computer labs, furnished units, and high-speed Internet access. High-speed Internet access is the most common and, in my view, soon to be required amenity provided in the student housing market. If a student housing property under consideration for acquisition is not equipped with some form of high-speed Internet access, the investor would be wise to factor in the cost of installing access into the building. Student housing apartment complexes without high-speed access to the Internet will suffer from a severe competitive disadvantage and cost the investor renters who'll choose not to live without it.

According to the NMHC survey, 87 percent of the properties surveyed indicated that high-speed Internet access is available at the student housing apartment building. It should come as no surprise that today's college student is high tech and wired for access to the Internet at a far greater rate than the population as a whole. According to Amy Raskin and Brad Lindenbaum of AllianceBernstein Institutional Investment Management, in "Broadband: The Revolution Underway," January 2004, only 22 percent of all U.S. households have high-speed Internet access accounts.

The top ten markets with the highest availability of high-speed Internet access in student housing apartments, according to the NMHC study, are:

Virginia Tech	100%
Colorado State University	97

The University of Tennessee	97
University of Kentucky	96
UNC–Chapel Hill	95
Appalachian State University (NC)	95
Western Michigan University	94
Auburn University (AL)	94
Georgia Southern University	94
Arizona State University	93

The NMHC Student Housing Survey also found the highest concentration of indicated student housing amenities at the following university campuses:

Amenity	University	Prevalence
Fitness Center	University of North Carolina	73%
Fitness Center	University of Texas	69
Fitness Center	University of Georgia	63
Fitness Center	University of California–Irvine	61
Fitness Center	University of South Carolina	57
Study Lounge	University of Texas	40
Study Lounge	Georgia Southern University	38
Study Lounge	University of South Carolina	27
Study Lounge	University of California–Irvine	26
Study Lounge	Arizona State University	24
Computer Lab	University of Texas	44
Computer Lab	University of Georgia	33
Computer Lab	University of Florida	33
Computer Lab	Arizona State University	32
Computer Lab	University of California–Irvine	26
Furnished Units	Penn State University	76
Furnished Units	Clemson University (SC)	69
Furnished Units	University of Maryland–College Park	69
Furnished Units	University of Arkansas–Fayetteville	64
Furnished Units	Auburn University	63

Increased amenities at a student housing property do not necessarily correspond to higher rents. In fact, the NMHC survey results illustrate that the West Coast, and in particular California where campus housing rents are the highest in the nation, don't have the most amenity-rich student housing properties.

DUE DILIGENCE REMINDER

While a real estate investment of any size requires extensive due diligence before committing funds, multifamily student housing investing especially requires research, confirmations, and analysis. Proceed with caution and reread the due diligence techniques discussed earlier and refer to the checklists in Appendix D before committing millions of dollars.

While experienced investors and lenders feel comfortable conducting inspections and analyzing the physical and financial condition of a particular investment, you still need to pay particular attention to the special considerations affecting the student housing real estate investment niche. Real estate investment firms specializing in the student housing niche that have recently gone public (more about the publicly traded REITs in the student housing market in Chapter 11) stress strong underwriting standards for all student housing apartment building acquisitions.

Educational Realty Trust (stock symbol EDR) discusses its acquisition strategy in various SEC filings. It's searching for well-located properties in markets that have stable or increasing student populations with an insufficient supply of student housing. While Educational Realty Trust (EDR) has targeted larger, garden-style apartment communities with rich amenities, its criteria for property and campus due diligence acquisitions are helpful for any serious investor to consider.

EDR considers the following factors before committing to an acquisition:

- Campus reputation
- Competitive admissions criteria
- Limited number of university-owned beds and limited expansion plans
- Distance of property from campus
- Property unit mix
- Competition
- Significant out-of-state enrollment
- Operating performance
- Potential for improved performance
- Ownership and capital structure
- Presence of desired amenities
- Maintenance of the property
- Access to university-sponsored or public transportation line
- Parking availability

Similarly, another public company specializing in the student housing niche, GMH Communities, has disclosed its multifamily student housing apartment investment criteria in SEC filings. GMH analyzes various factors including the following:

- The ability to increase rents and maximize cash flows
- The terms of existing and proposed leases
- Comparisons of proposed rents to market rents
- Creditworthiness of student residents and parent guarantors
- Local demographic and college and university enrollment trends
- Occupancy of and demand for similar properties
- Population and rental rate trends
- The ability to lease or sublease any unoccupied space
- The ability of the property to achieve long-term capital appreciation
- The ability of the property to produce cash flow for current distributions

- The age, location, and projected residual value of the property
- The ability to expand and network relationships at the targeted university

8

PRIVATELY OWNED DORMS AND PUBLIC-PRIVATE PARTNERSHIPS

PRIVATELY OWNED DORMS

As previously mentioned, the private multifamily student housing market on just about every major campus consists of apartment properties. While these properties contain modern amenities, they greatly differ from traditional university-owned dorms. Private student housing properties, for the most part, don't include an on-site food-service or meal-plan option. In addition, private campus housing comes with no residence hall advisor, or RA, to watch over the college students.

A hybrid type of student housing property is the privately owned dormitory. Located on campuses across America, they're approved and monitored by the university housing office for minimum standards. These privately owned dormitories are increasingly filling the gap between growing enrollments and university-owned dormitory beds. Although rules and regulations are part of any apartment lease (and student housing leases commonly carry antiparty provisions, rules, and restrictions), those required in private student housing leases pale in comparison to university-owned dorms.

Highly Specialized Business

The operation of university-approved, privately owned dormitories can be a lucrative real estate investment on large-enrollment campuses that require lowerclassmen to live in approved dorms. With a built-in renter base, many private dormitory operators achieve high occupancy levels and realize tremendous cash flow. In this highly specialized business, unique management and operational skills are required. To maintain university-approved certification, you're required to provide services similar to those in the university setting. For example, according to certification requirements, a food-service department must offer three meals a day, residence advisors have to live on each floor, security levels are high, and extensive resident rules are applied. Losing this certification status could clearly devastate the income stream and value of a privately owned dormitory.

Private dorms offer a more luxurious (and more expensive) living arrangement for those students (or parents) willing to spend more for dorm living. Most private dormitories provide air-conditioning, semiprivate bathrooms, and upgraded food service. As an alternative to university-owned dorms, private dorms satisfy requirements to live on campus in an approved dorm while meeting the students' desire for amenities. As a result of the cost differences between public and private dorms, private ones tend to be the home of choice for the "rich kids" on campus.

Private dormitory deals tend to fall into two categories:

1. Aging, dilapidated smaller properties suffering from poor occupancy and requiring major capital improvements, and

2. High-occupancy properties near the center of campus, offered at high prices and requiring the ability to put together a single deal of $20 million or more.

Investing in the student housing market by buying private dormitories is *not* for the inexperienced or unsophisticated real estate investor. As noted previously, its success hinges on the university's housing department maintaining official approval. Substantial restrictions and inspections are imposed on the private dorms by the university housing office. Food service and residence advisors (RAs) are certain to be required to maintain the university's official seal of approval. Safety and access standards must also be met.

One downside to private dormitory ownership (compared to private student housing apartments) is the lease term. While just about every private student housing apartment lease covers a 12-month term despite the fact that the unit is vacant all summer, university rules require dorms to offer 9-month school term leases. That means no revenue is generated in the summer. Because of the unique challenges faced by the private student dormitory owner, and the many required non–real estate services, private dormitory real estate deals are very hard to finance.

Be Cautious!

If the thought of investing in and owning privately owned dorms makes you nervous, it should! I've stayed away from them. Still, many large companies and private investor groups do well owning these dorms. They hire expert third-party managers to maintain stringent university-imposed standards. I say: Best of luck to them and I wish them continued success. If you decide to own privately owned dorms, you won't have any competition from me!

PUBLIC-PRIVATE PARTNERSHIPS

Public-private partnerships have become increasingly common in the student housing business. They're fueled by public funding shortages, coupled with the increased need for on-campus student housing—especially to house the increased numbers of freshmen required to live in university-owned dorms. By teaming with private sector developers and investors, universities have begun to solve their money problems and have found willing partners in new dormitory construction. Universities have attracted these partners by donating university-owned land and providing tax-exempt bond financing for construction.

The still-evolving public-private joint venture student housing market typically falls into one of four categories:

1. A traditional partnership with the university owning the land and building, providing all the capital and managing the finished dormitory but hiring a private student housing developer to manage the construction of the building.

2. A partially private deal with the land owned and donated by the university on a ground lease to a private student housing developer that builds, manages, and finances the student housing building. The university receives a ground lease fee and the private developer retains the balance of the property's net operating income.

3. To take advantage of low-rate financing, the university donates the land to a university-affiliated, not-for-profit foundation and finances the project using tax-exempt bonds. At the same time, a private, third-party student housing developer constructs the property for a fee. Then a private, third-party management company manages the finished student housing property on behalf of the foundation for a fee.

4. Similar to the previous option, the land is transferred to a not-for-profit entity. However, in this category the not-for-profit is not affiliated with the university.

A public-private partnership for a student housing project usually features the built-in advantage of a great location. No private property owner owns more, or better located, land on major campuses than the university itself. If the university contributes a prime close-in site for the development of a student housing project, one can be assured of high occupancy when the property is built and becomes available for rent.

As the student housing shortage grows against the backdrop of state budget cuts, public-private joint venture partnerships will continue to evolve and grow in popularity on major university campuses.

A Contractor's Christmas in August

Every August, it's like Christmas for each college town handyman, painter, and carpet company. While most retailers do the majority of their business and make the most profit during December's holiday shopping season, in the college housing business, August is turnover month. Each August (except for the minority of campuses that turn over student housing leases in May), every rental apartment must be made ready for the new lease. While trash bins overflow from the move out, maintenance and repair crews descend on student housing apartment complexes to make the units ready for the new residents in a short number of days.

I visited one of our student housing apartment properties at the University of Illinois on the Sunday after the expiring lease tenants had moved out and just before the Friday all of the new student leases were to begin. I was in the Champaign, Illinois, area and decided to drive by our building, managed by a local student housing property management firm. It was on Sunday at around 5 PM. I expected to see an empty building with an empty garage. Instead, I witnessed college turnover week in full swing.

With so many apartments to paint, carpets to lay, and minor repairs to complete in a short time frame, the building buzzed with tradespeople. You would have thought they were making the property ready for a visit by the president of the United States. It was great to see that our outside management firm rallied the troops and had everyone busy at work on Sunday night. These guys were on the verge of having a huge month. The maintenance and repair crews were busy finishing up our building so they could move on to the next, making thousands of apartments ready for the new academic term in a matter of days.

Turnover week is a strange sight to see—it's almost like a convention hotel getting rooms ready in a whirlwind after a large checkout in anticipation of new conventioneers checking in the same day. The difference in the student housing business is that every wall and ceiling gets patched and repainted and lots of carpet gets replaced. The cleaning crew comes in after the major work is completed and all of the units are made to look new in a short time.

Although the cost of damage repair to the apartment is recovered from the vacating student's security deposits, painting and other turnover costs are expensed at a student housing property in a single month. That's why the repair guys have a great month. You'll never see them take a vacation in August.

9

CONDOMINIUM DEVELOPMENT NEAR CAMPUS

THE COLLEGE TOWN CONDOMINIUM MARKET

As investors get more comfortable and sophisticated in the student housing property niche, multifamily condominium development projects in college towns will grow in popularity. There has already been a start in that direction, yet it's still not widespread. Condominium projects are being developed near major university campuses in response to growing housing shortages and the trend to own rather than to rent.

CONDOMINIUM OWNERSHIP

While the national trend in increased condominium ownership at the expense of apartment rentals may be because of the availability of low-rate mortgages, still, the condominium market is here to stay, and it's affecting the college town apartment market.

Commissions and Long-term Relationships Go Together

Although my firm, partner, and I carry real estate brokers' licenses and are active members of Realtor organizations, we don't act as brokers for third parties. We only buy and sell for our own account; our one-and-only client is ourselves.

Being Realtors gives us access to networking opportunities with other Realtors. Many real estate brokers, who are our friends and professional colleagues, bring us deals—often before they get exposed to a wider group of buyers.

In this business, your fellow real estate brokers become your best friends and should always be treated fairly. They make a living facilitating property transactions and earning commissions. I never let paying a real estate commission hinder making a deal. There is far more to be earned on a successful real estate acquisition than letting an outside brokerage commission stand in the way. We never even flinch or try to negotiate down a real estate commission. Why? Because in this long-haul business, we always want brokers to call us first when a property within our investment niche becomes available for sale.

Because of my close relationship with an active, high-volume investment property broker in Chicago—enhanced by our reputation for quickly closing transactions without cumbersome contingencies—the first call a broker made on an apartment building deal that had to close in 30 days was to me. The owner had insisted that the transaction remain confidential and unannounced to the property's tenants and custodian. Because the owner didn't want the property exposed to the market with lots of property showings, he was willing to sell at a discount for a discreet and quick noncontingent deal.

When the broker described the building, the location, and the gross annual income, I knew I was being handed a gift. After a quick property inspection, I submitted a contract for the full asking price along with a nonrefundable check for $100,000 in earnest money. Although we could have easily sold the property on our own without a commission, a year later we gave the listing to the same broker, at a full commission, and we sold the property for $400,000 more than our purchase price. That shows we're in this business for the long haul.

Relationships are everything in the real estate investment game; it's not a one-transaction industry. And this approach pays! Guess who gets the first call from the broker when the next underpriced deal comes along?

There are many compelling reasons for consumers to own their own condominiums rather than rent apartments. Although college living is, by definition, temporary and transient—which favors renting rather than owning—the real estate investor can't ignore the reasons students and their parents have for owning condominiums nor the effect that ownership will have on student housing markets.

In a historic low-rate mortgage environment that features special financing with low down payments and interest-only payments, condominium ownership has become available to an increasingly large pool of potential owners. With monthly payments at or below apartment rents and mortgage interest payments being tax deductible, condo ownership can be far more attractive than renting. Particularly in high rent areas such as major college campuses, it's often cheaper to own a condominium than rent an apartment with similar amenities, taking into account the tax advantages.

Furthermore, aside from monthly payment savings, condominium ownership allows owners to build equity and create wealth rather than having nothing but rent receipts to show after years of leasing an apartment. And as you know, ownership also creates the opportunity to realize an investment return based on the historical rate of appreciation enjoyed by residential real estate.

Well-located and high-amenity buildings typically command the highest rents. In the case of campus rental properties, new properties close to the center of campus rent for the highest rates and enjoy the highest levels of occupancy. Condo ownership costs usually compare most favorably when the alternative is a high-rent, well-located apartment property.

National Association of Realtors (NAR) statistics show that in 2004, appreciation rates for condominiums surpassed those for single-family homes and this trend is expected to continue. By buying a condominium in a well-located, growing market, an owner can reap the benefits of anticipated appreciation in values. In addition, condominium buildings tend to remain better kept and expertly maintained than apartment buildings because of the residents' pride of ownership.

Astute apartment dwellers looking to lower their after-tax housing expense and create greater wealth would be wise to purchase a well-located condominium near a major university campus. Given the many favorable financing options available, coupled with the potential for significant appreciation, this is a great time to purchase a condominium rather than rent long-term.

Potential University-Town Condominium Buyers

The potential market for both new construction and conversion condominium developments on major college campuses has a likelihood of success because of the increased number of potential condominium buyers in the university market. University employees, local company executives, seniors, health-care professionals, and parents of students are all potential buyers of condominium units at or near major university campuses. Within my company's condominium development and conversion business unit, we've found that where a sufficient number of consumers want to live, there's always a market, at some price level, for condominium sales and profit. As universities—and the consumers they attract—continue to grow, the market for campus condominiums will follow.

University and Local Town Employees

One thing is for certain: Over the next few decades, major universities will get bigger, resulting in increased numbers of employees to serve the growing student population. In addition to the universities themselves, it's become common for major companies to locate near campuses to take advantage of university research and brainpower, and bring innovative products and services to market. As university business parks grow, the base of private sector professionals living in college towns will increase as well.

In addition, many major universities in America have medical schools and large medical teaching hospitals as part of the curriculum. The size of the affiliated hospital medical and support staff will grow as student enrollment increases in the medical schools. Aside from the growth of the medical schools, health-care providers continue to be one of the highest growth sectors in the national economy. The demand on the health-care system will increase with the growth in the student, university, and private sector population, resulting in further private sector employment growth.

Parents of Students

As more students come of college age and more parents seek real estate investment opportunities, the market for sales of campus condominiums to parents will expand. Faced with increasingly high student housing apartment rents for well-located student housing properties, many parents recognize the financial advantages of owning a condominium for their sons or daughters to live in during the college enrollment years. As mentioned in Chapter 6, disadvantages and caveats must be addressed when buying a condominium in a college town, but there's no denying that the market for sales to parents exists. Savvy real estate entrepreneurs, real estate developers, and investors ought to be ready to take advantage of it!

Retirees

Yes, you read it correctly; retirees are growing potential condominium buyers. Retirees, especially alumni, seeking to locate back near their campuses have been a trend and the subject of some recent national press. According to *Urban Land* (May 2005), the official publication of the Urban Land Institute, a growing niche real estate investment opportunity is to be found in the growing trend of retirees nationwide seeking to pack up for retirement and return to live on or near campus.

In fact, so many Stanford University alums have exhibited this desire that Classic Residence by Hyatt has recently built a retirement community on land leased from Stanford near campus. The trend has become so common that, to date, approximately 50 such retirement communities have been built on or near major university campuses across the country. According to the Urban Land Institute, at least another 25 similar college-affiliated communities are either under construction or in the planning stages. This is a trend that is here to stay and growing.

Retirees, especially alumni, are the perfect win-win situation for major universities. They have access to the cultural, entertainment, and learning opportunities available in major university towns. At the same time, universities have renewed special access to a population uniquely qualified to see the advantages of the school and make financial commitments to endowments and capital campaign drives. Universities love retired alumni with money to bequest, and retired alumni love to feel young again, rejoining the college community they loved in their more vibrant years!

Recent successful retiree condominium developments near major university campuses have sold out quickly. Built in 2001, the University Commons project adjacent to the University of Michigan in Ann Arbor consists of a 92-unit town house and condominium new-construction development, with apartments ranging in price from $200,000 to $600,000. The Ann Arbor is an independent living senior facility with beautiful grounds and close ties to university-provided lectures and cultural events. Another, and larger, successful retirement condominium community is the 2003-built, independent living property named The Village at Penn

Retired Boomers Won't Be Sitting Around

U.S. Census Bureau population figures indicate that 13 percent of the population, or 35 million people, are already more than 65 years of age. By 2030, when the tail end of the baby boomers have reached 65, it's estimated that more than 20 percent of the total population will be retirement age. This group of retirees won't be satisfied to sit around all day playing cards or watching television. College campus retirement condominiums will increasingly appeal to the boomers. You watch and see!

State. Located on 80 acres of land one mile from the center of the Penn State campus, this property features one-bedroom and two-bedroom condominium units priced from $161,000 to $361,000.

The echo boomers are turning college age in massive numbers over the next several years and creating the predicted student housing shortages over the next decade. But it's their parents, the baby boomers, who are creating a population bump in the number of individuals entering retirement age. As people live longer, college town retirement options and senior condominium developments will appeal to increasingly large numbers of consumers as a retirement option. People born between 1946 and 1964 are the most involved, active, and intellectually active generation ever to reach retirement age. The lure of condominiums close to campus has a unique appeal. For the astute real estate investor/developer, retiree condominium developments make up yet another opportunity within the college campus multifamily apartment real estate niche.

Location Outside the Core of Campuses

Unlike traditional rental student housing niche opportunities, college town condominium developments are not necessarily more desirable when located close to the center of campus. While students like to be in the middle of the action, including the campus town nightlife and entertainment (by the way, Thursday is now considered the beginning of the weekend on most college campuses), potential buyers for campus condominiums may prefer a location outside of the core. Most currently successful campus condominium developments tend to be *near* campus, but off of it in a garden-style or town house construction.

Obviously, all real estate transactions must be regarded as unique. Each deal and each campus has its own set of peculiarities. But, generally, I'm not a fan of putting a condominium project right in the center of campus, and I don't see that happening in a big way.

New Construction—Not for the Inexperienced

Today, most condominium and town house campus developments are newly constructed and highly sophisticated, requiring a great deal of experience and deep financial pockets. While an excellent niche market for an experienced developer in the new-construction condominium business on college campuses exists, this area is absolutely not recommended for inexperienced investors. Don't worry whether you qualify—without the required experience, no matter how much money is out there, nobody will finance your project!

CONDOMINIUM CONVERSION

As surmised with close-in student housing apartment building opportunities in Chapter 7, I recognize an opportunity for the rehab of older garden-style and town house properties near major university campuses for conversion to condominiums. Many college towns have aging, tired apartment and town house complexes, built largely in the 1960s and 1970s a mile or two off of campus. Most need a rehab makeover. By remodeling and repositioning these properties, you can resell the individual units as condominiums at a substantial profit if they can be purchased at the correct price.

For those investors with experience rehabbing apartment properties, or condominium conversions in other markets, college markets may provide yet another market of opportunity. If you have the experience and ability to handle condominium conversions in one market, you might want to get in the car and check out neighboring college campuses. Certainly, large campuses within close proximity to your home base of rehab and condominium conversion activities are worth exploring. I'm comfortable with rehab and condominium conversions, having completed many such projects, and I'm less concerned with the potential for failure on a conversion project than on a new construction. If the condos don't sell, or rehab estimates come in higher than originally figured, you can fall back on holding the building as a student housing rental property.

Condominium Development Analysis

The financial analysis and due diligence required to "pull the trigger" on a condominium development differs significantly from that needed for a rental property investment. While all of the factors external to the building itself remain the same, including examining the strengths and growth prospects of the university, the project itself needs to be examined differently. While a rental property investment opportunity lives or dies based on property cash flow and net operating income (as discussed in Chapter 5), a condominium development project is operated by the individual owners, not the developer.

Working the Numbers of a Condominium Development

In my experience, the best way to underwrite the financial aspects of a potential condominium development—new construction or conversion—is from the top down. Always start with the anticipated gross selling prices of the finished project condominiums to be offered to the market. The total gross selling price of all of the condominium units in a development is called the gross sellout. To determine the end selling prices, make the effort to perform an extensive survey of the condominium market in the local community. When it comes to determining realistic and actual ultimate gross sellout prices, there is no substitute for the professional advice of a high-volume local real estate agent familiar with condo selling prices. Most real estate agents are happy to provide their opinion of the market value selling prices for a potential condominium project in exchange for the opportunity to receive an exclusive listing agreement once the project comes to market.

Once you have a good projection of the gross sellout, you can determine the expense side of the condominium development. Expenses of condominium development—new or conversion—to be deducted from the gross sellout include:

- The initial cost of the property
- Construction or rehab costs
- Real estate sales commissions
- Interest carrying costs
- Various soft costs, including legal, closing, and miscellaneous reports

Once you deduct the condominium project costs from the gross sellout, you can determine the condominium development's net potential profit. Most experienced condominium developers look for a minimum profit margin of at least 15 percent before they give the green light for the project. The percentage profit margin is based on the gross sellout. For example, if the gross sellout is $5 million, a 15 percent profit margin would equal a net profit (gross sellout minus all expenses) on the deal of $750,000.

In my opinion, there's simply too much risk when it comes to condominium development to go into a deal with any less than a potential 15 percent profit margin. While some developers are satisfied with a lower profit margin, I like to cover the potential for higher rehab and construction costs and/or lower gross selling prices. With a margin that's too thin, you have no room for any error in your initial financial projections.

10

UNIQUE RISK FACTORS FOR MANAGEMENT AND OPERATIONS

Operating apartment rental properties isn't easy. Comparing various types of real estate (office, retail, and industrial), I think residential rental real estate is the most intensive to manage. Apartment building renters, unlike office or retail tenants, are renting their home from a landlord. People spend a lot of time in their apartment and use the bedrooms, living rooms, bathrooms, and kitchens seven days a week sometimes without a break. Toilets often back up, mechanical systems fail, and the heat and air-conditioning system can break down. When a tenant has a problem in a residential rental unit, it's almost always an emergency.

Traditional apartment rental property operations and management is tough enough. Add 18-year-old to 21-year-old student residents away from Mom and Dad on a large college campus to the mix, and the building owner has to face up to some real challenges. If properly managed and operated, a student housing property can be a cash cow and create great wealth. But if improperly managed, a student housing property investment can be a disaster. By recognizing the challenges you face in the student housing niche, prudent investors can be prepared to address problems and protect the value of their property.

REAL ESTATE INDUSTRY RISK FACTORS

I'm a great cheerleader of the real estate investment business; I can think of no business I'd rather be in. And I know many people who've become multimillionaires in this business. At the same time, I deplore those who would have anyone believe that the real estate investment business is without risks. In fact, the only way to stay ahead of risk is to recognize the potential traps and manage them effectively. If you're new to the business, step into it with your eyes wide open. If you're a seasoned professional with real estate investment experience, be on guard and remain vigilant.

General Economic Conditions

General economic conditions can have a positive or negative effect on the real estate investment business. For example, the state of the economy affects lenders' appetites for financing, investors' tolerance for equity investments in assets such as real estate, and consumers' tolerance for rent increases. The residential real estate rental industry as a whole is more affected by negative general economic conditions than the student housing niche. While, for example, traditional multifamily apartment property rent growth and occupancy levels are closely tied to the unemployment rate, student housing property rent growth and occupancy don't move with employment numbers. Generally, the larger the number of people in the workforce, the higher the occupancy levels and the rents in traditional apartment properties. Rent growth in student housing properties is tied to enrollment growth and available campus housing.

Rising Interest Rates

Rising interest rates almost always affect the real estate investment market. Many investment real estate transactions only make sense—based on the purchase price and underlying property cash flow—at lower levels of interest rates for mortgages. The same real estate investment property transaction may fall apart and not get financed in a high interest rate environment. These environments require greater net operating income and property cash flow than low interest rate ones because lenders need to feel comfortable that you can adequately service the debt.

However, residential rental investment properties sometimes run counter to conventional wisdom when it comes to the interest rate environment. When interest rates are low, alternatives to renting an apartment—i.e., owning a detached single-family home or a condominium—appeal to consumers. Consequently, in a low interest rate environment, apartment building vacancy rates run high and landlords reduce rents or provide incentives to lease up their buildings. Conversely, when mortgage interest rates are high, fewer people are attracted to home-ownership and fewer consumers qualify for financing; thus the size of the renter pool goes up. With more consumers looking to rent apartments when interest rates are high, occupancy levels jump and rents increase. The result is greater net operating income and cash flow for apartment building owners and increased property values *despite* higher interest rates. Remember, I told you this isn't a simple business!

Competitive Property Risk

With any property investment, you risk facing the competition of new properties coming to the market. Newer and better buildings are constantly being developed and can render what was once a class A property into an aging and tired product. A good insurance policy against being one-upped by a shiny new building up the street is to buy a property below the building's replacement cost. The new building owner needs to cover the investment with rental rates that support today's construction cost. By acquiring an asset below today's construction cost, you'll have a competitive rental price advantage to keep your property at a high occupancy level.

Delinquent Rent Collection

The inability to collect rents in a timely manner from tenants is another real estate investment property risk. It's a fact of life that when people hit hard times and money is tight, renters can be slow in paying the rent. Generally speaking, residential rent tends to be paid as a priority because people need places to live. So rather than risk eviction, a tenant will pay the apartment rent and skip a payment to the credit card company or other creditor. It's wise to use good credit-checking practices and confirm employment when screening prospective tenants. This helps you protect your income stream as the owner of a residential rental property.

Vacant Space

Additionally, all real estate investment properties risk not being able to rent all the available space or meet the projected rental rate objectives. Every residential real estate investment transaction needs to be underwritten with some reasonable vacancy factor figured in as a cost. This business is far too risky to project 100 percent occupancy, even for the best located of investment properties. Face it, undesirable units with poor views or old kitchen appliances simply may not rent so quickly or for so high a rental rate as do superior units.

Inability to Control Operating Expenses

While all investors—regardless of experience and sophistication levels—attempt to project future operating expenses for a property, projections are as much art as science. One can never know with absolute certainty exactly what operating expenses will run next year, let alone five years out. Many building operating expenses escalate for reasons beyond the control of the property owner, and better management can't reduce certain costs. Real estate investors have recently seen substantial increases in heating fuel costs, insurance premiums, and real estate taxes that couldn't have possibly been quantified precisely just a few years ago when building operating cost projections were made.

Government Regulation

An increasing array of government regulations and codes has become the norm in the residential investment property business. Building and zoning codes may require large expenditures to come into compliance. Environmental cleanup costs, often hidden, may require a large expenditure. And when a property is substantially remodeled, the cost of complying with the Americans with Disabilities Act (ADA) can be staggering. Furthermore, local government registration, licensing fees, and inspection costs can add greatly to building operating costs.

Terrorist Risk

A new risk inherent in all real estate investment transactions that must be faced in the aftermath of September 11, 2001 is the risk of future terrorist attacks. Further terrorist attacks in the United States can severely harm the market for and value of investment real estate. High-profile trophy properties are more likely to be terrorist targets. They may become unmarketable without the ability to attract tenants, lenders, or buyers. Future terrorist attacks would likely drive up insurance and security costs on all real estate investment properties. I hate to think or write about terrorism's risk to the real estate investment business. Unfortunately, this very real risk needs to be recognized in the 21st century.

Illiquidity of Investment

A risk that applies to all real estate investment property is that real estate remains a relatively illiquid investment. Real estate has become a popular and sought-after investment vehicle. However, it's a nontraditional asset class without a highly liquid market once the investor decides to exit the business.

Unlike shares on the New York Stock Exchange, an investor can't decide to sell out and turn a building into cash with a quick call to his or her stockbroker. Real estate investment property assets take months to market and liquidate.

The student housing investment property niche carries special risk factors that need to be recognized. By adequately addressing them, you can limit the downside in a student housing investment. Ignore these risk factors and you will almost certainly lose money, perhaps lots of it!

UNIQUE STUDENT HOUSING NICHE CHALLENGES

The standard nightmare flashes in every reasonable investor's mind when hearing the words "student housing." It's a vision of excessive property damage, including large holes through the apartment drywall. If this scares you off, trust me, in the chapters that follow I'll win you back over to the idea of investing in the student housing niche. Thank goodness, the reality of student residents' care for the property is far better than your nightmare.

Okay, now I'm redeeming the student housing industry as an excellent way to make lots of money in real estate. Let me push the envelope and test your tolerance for all of the risks you'll encounter. By confronting the special challenges facing this niche, you can manage and operate around the problems. Although I can't guarantee that what follows includes every possible unique problem you'll face as a student housing property owner, I've hit the highlights.

1. Higher Capital Expenditure Reserves

Student housing rental properties—while not the stereotype of the popular movie *Animal House*—still require greater reserves for capital expenditures than do traditional apartment properties. That's why it's imperative that you put aside sufficient reserves each year to fund replacements and upgrades to the physical structure of the building.

When our company makes a student housing property purchase, we fund an up-front capital reserve account at closing and add to the capital reserve account each year based on the size and condition of the property.

Many student housing properties, depending on the particular college market, include furnished apartments as the expected standard. Where properties include furnishings, you also need to plan and budget for a furniture replacement schedule.

2. Limited Availability of Insurance Coverage

Enough proper insurance coverage is needed to protect any real estate investment against loss—and protect owners from liability claims. Student housing is not a universally understood investment property class and, as a result, only a limited number of insurance companies write coverage for it. Experienced insurance brokers who expose properties to willing carriers are especially important in the student housing niche market. They know how to adequately cover risk and minimize premium costs.

3. Short Leasing Cycle

While a well-located student housing property on a major university campus can enjoy high occupancy levels (approaching 100 percent), you actually have a short leasing window in which to fully lease up the property. If the property operator can't lease up the units in the building before the academic year starts, it's unlikely that the remaining units will get rented. The short leasing window puts tremendous pressure on early marketing and leasing efforts to ensure a full building when classes begin in the fall.

4. Third-Party Management

In the student housing real estate niche it's often wise to hire third-party management firms familiar and active in the local college market to lease up and manage the property. Unless the targeted property is very large, it often doesn't pay for an out-of-town real estate investor to hire an on-site manager. Selecting the right manager for the property—one with a keen understanding of the market for lease-up—is key to building a successful investment opportunity. If you've hired a poorly performing management company and the property has a high number of vacancies after the leasing season is over, it's unlikely that cash flow will increase until the next academic year and leasing season.

5. Creditworthiness of Tenants

Obviously, college students are unique tenants when it comes to documenting their ability to pay rent. Most students have either no, or very low, income and depend either on funding from parents or student loans to pay their expenses. For these reasons, our company prefers parental guarantees on leases and joint-and-several liability of all occupants of the apartment unit to pay all of the rent due rather than a limited by-the-bed student housing lease.

6. Joint-and-Several versus By-the-Bed Leases

Under a joint-and-several liability lease, roommates are each responsible for paying the total rental obligation. If one of the roommates has a credit or cash flow problem, the others must pick up the slack and make sure the total rent gets paid. Under the by-the-bed method of leasing student housing properties, each student is only responsible for his or her own prorated share of the rent, based on the number of beds in the apartment. For example, under a by-the-bed lease arrangement of a four-bedroom, four-roommate apartment unit, each student renter is responsible for 25 percent of the total rental obligation.

By-the-bed leases typically result in higher per-unit and per-square-foot rental rates than similar joint-and-several liability leased units. Despite the potential for a slight increase in rent in exchange for the limitation of a student renter's potential liability, for my money—and for the protection of my investors' and lenders' money—we prefer being joint-and-several liability landlords. Large firms entering the student housing market owning big student housing complexes nationally are moving to by-the-bed leases. They use this type of lease as a selling point and solicit parental endorsement along with guarantees. Personally, I don't think a trend toward a by-the-bed lease arrangement is worthwhile because it takes a lot more time, effort, and expense to fill more beds, manage more leases, and collect more rents than with joint-and-several arrangements.

7. Turnover Costs

Student housing properties have an unusual characteristic: They turn over the entire tenant base every single year, with 100 percent of the tenants signing new leases at the same time.

Leases tend to begin with the beginning of the academic year while apartments need to be made ready for the new fall occupancy at the same time. Because of the more-intense-than-typical wear and tear, most student housing units need to be painted each year and carpets cleaned or replaced. Walls need patching and apartments need to be professionally cleaned. Turnover costs are an important consideration in projecting and budgeting for a student housing investment property. Remember, you'll likely recover much of the cost of turnover from student security deposits.

8. Security Deposits

Lease security deposits are an integral part of the student housing rental property business. Security deposits ensure that all lease-end obligations are paid and that the property can be adequately prepared for subsequent tenants. Although all tenants, including students, deserve to be treated fairly by landlords when it comes to security deposits, having properly documented charge-backs for security deposits and the resulting income from security deposit forfeiture is important when running a profitable investment property.

9. Prepaid Rent

Student housing properties, by definition, provide a unique rent collection challenge. While leases cover 12-month occupancy, student housing property is only actually occupied for 9 or 10 months. Although some schools have active summer school enrollments, most students return home during the summer months and college towns tend to clear out.

As a result, it's common in the student housing business to collect summer rental payments in advance. Leases that begin in August usually require the payment of 12 equal monthly rental installments to begin the previous June. This prepayment policy assures that the new occupants pay rent before they move in and receive a key. The prepaid rental also ensures that the last several months' rent are paid even though the student occupants won't be in town or reachable for rent collection. A well-designed prepaid rent and security deposit policy, consistent with competitive structures within a particular market, makes a student housing property much less likely to experience collection and delinquency losses than a traditional rental property building.

10. Self-Management versus Third-Party Management

Any residential property investment presents the owners with the decision about self-managing the property or hiring a third-party management firm. Student housing properties require special attention to this important decision. Third-party management firms add cost to the operation of the property in the form of management fees. In my experience, unless the property is within a city where the investor owns and self-manages other properties— or unless the property is large (100 units or more)—it's usually prudent to hire an experienced professional student housing property manager. Once the investor owns a sufficient number of units within any given student housing market, it may then be worth considering taking over management directly and hiring a full-time staff.

Selecting a third-party management firm is one of the single most important decisions made in the student housing investment property business. The firm you choose needs to be good at the day-to-day management and monthly reporting systems. It must also possess special skills required to lease up the entire property within a short window of the academic year leasing cycle.

I recommend you meet in person with your potential management firm choices in a particular college town. Look at their track records, see their office locations and computer systems, view sample reports provided on managed properties, and drive by other properties the firms manage.

In every college town I've surveyed or considered investing in, I find two or three easily identifiable firms that specialize in student housing rentals. Check out the ads in the student newspaper and drive the campus area noting the management company names on signs of other close-in student rental properties. I guarantee that within ten minutes you'll have your list of student housing management firms to interview.

ENROLLMENT INCREASES EUPHORIA

A major university campus with a large student population and a plan for enrollment increases is a dream come true for a student housing investor. However, if you find such a dream college town, don't ignore other important data. The ratio of university-owned beds to students, as we have discussed, is a key ratio to consider.

If the planned enrollment increases are especially large and you find yourself excited about the future prospects of your planned student housing investment and an increasingly tight supply of available student housing, slow down and do your homework. Remember, you're not the only real estate entrepreneur looking for student housing opportunities. Many investors, including new construction builders and developers, seek investment opportunities of their own. The bigger the planned enrollment increase and the lower the university-owned-beds-to-student ratio, the greater the attraction of new construction student housing buildings.

Especially watch out if the enrollment increase numbers are unusually good. Count on the campus being recognized by all the players in the industry and a new large student housing complex coming soon to campus. Survey the current privately owned student housing stock and research new or planned construction projects, especially on a "dream come true" campus.

Kids Will Be Kids

It's often possible to get so caught up in the numbers and calculations of a student housing investment that you forget the bottom line. Remember, you're renting an apartment or house to a group of students who are concentrated in an environment with other college students, away from home with no parental supervision. It shouldn't come as a shock that some students party too much and drink a lot. It's imperative that student housing property owners provide for the adequate safety and well-being of residents. Security such as proper locking devices and peepholes, balconies that support beer kegs, and smoke and fire alarm devices need to be provided and maintained. On-call security and party patrol services need to be a part of the owner's or third-party management firm's arsenal of available vendors. Face the realities of college life.

Significant Competition

Prudent student housing investors know that with significant opportunity comes significant competition. The universities themselves may decide to build more dormitory rooms to meet demand on a particular college campus. In addition, the student housing market has seen the recent public offerings of three real estate investment trusts (see Chapter 11) dedicated specifically to making investments in the student housing niche. Institutional investors are poised to place hundreds of millions of dollars into real estate investments in this niche. In addition, private real estate investment firms and individuals are getting ready to enter the business and are searching for student housing investments.

Changing Admissions and Housing Policies

Although favorable demographics pointing to echo boomers coming to college campuses in droves is undeniable, there can be no guarantee that a particular university will increase the size of its enrollment. While public universities are pressured to provide advanced educational degrees to the growing population, a particular school may decide to cap or limit its enrollment. In addition, at campuses with a surplus of unoccupied, university-owned dorm rooms, the official housing policy at a particular school could change to require freshman and sophomores to live in university-approved dormitories.

Enrollment Decreases

Do you see that a growing potential college student population size doesn't automatically translate into an increased enrollment at a particular university? Institutions of higher learning see fluctuations from year to year in the number of applications for new admissions. Although, generally, the application pool at most universities has increased each year, there's no assurance that a particular school won't see a drop in applications or enrollments. A downgrade in academic ranking, scandals, or other negative publicity can cause interest in enrollment to fall at a particular university.

Changing Student Demographics

While echo boomers are definitely attending college in record numbers (as seen from a close look at the demographic data in Part One), the increase in the population size turning 18 is not equally distributed throughout the nation. There are many high growth and stable population states, but some states have negative population growth projections. In addition, there can be no guarantee that increases in the size of the population will continue in the currently projected high growth states. For example, I don't see the population falling out of love with the southern sun states, but no one has a crystal ball that can predict with certainty that this trend will continue for ten years or more.

If You Don't Like Seeing Beer Cans, This Isn't for You

Touring a student housing property is not the same as looking at a traditional multifamily apartment building. We've become accustomed to the drill, but I remember our feelings when we first entered the student housing niche and started visiting apartments occupied by 20-year-olds living away from home without any parents around.

Prepare yourself. You're wise to become immune to signs of underage drinking. If the sight of empty beer bottles, unreturned kegs and taps, and Budweiser posters is a problem for you, you shouldn't seriously look at an occupied student housing apartment building. Additionally, if erotic posters and stolen city street signs bother you as apartment interior decorating, this may not be the field for you.

I hate to generalize or destroy your image of students at the most selective colleges and universities in the country, but after touring hundreds of college student apartments, I must confess that our future world leaders—both male and female—tend to be total slobs. There is no such thing as a dirty laundry basket in most student housing apartments. Clothes don't get hung up, beds rarely get made, and empty (or not completely empty) pizza boxes serve as permanent decoration on the living room floor. Students have an affinity for big-screen televisions, video games, and lots of shot glasses. I've rarely met college students who care if you walk into their apartments with a property manager or listing broker unannounced. Once they realize you're not with the building or campus security, they loosen up.

Today's atmosphere on every major university campus across the country is supercasual. Forget casual business dress or the blue jeans look. Gym shorts, sweatpants, no shoes or socks, and no shirts (for the males!) are the standard dress code when hanging out in a student apartment. This supercasual atmosphere actually allows for easy conversation. My partner, Barbara, has become skilled at getting the "real story" on any student housing property from student residents. College kids "tell it like it is," rarely holding back information. For that reason, we love it when all the residents are home during a property tour.

Once you get into the student housing business, you'll see what I mean and learn to chill out. Uptight business types don't conduct the best property tours and due diligence inspections. We like the laid-back atmosphere and have learned to tour properties in our casual blue jeans or casual slacks outfits. I am sure we still look like parents to the students, but it makes us feel as if we're blending into the atmosphere.

We also have a college-age-looking associate who loves hanging around campuses, talking to students at other competing student housing buildings, and getting the straight scoop on market rents as well as students' opinions about the desirability of a potential property acquisition. In fact, when we all dress and act casually—and kid around on our property tours—we're more approachable to the students and obtain better information about our potential acquisition than if we appeared as stuffy, dressed-up businesspeople.

You've now been officially warned and know most of the areas to be cautious of, although I can't guarantee I caught all of the potential traps to watch out for. As promised, it's time to build up your confidence and show you why student housing can be the next great thing in real estate investing for you!

11

STUDENT HOUSING NICHE COMES OF AGE

When the history books covering real estate investment property are written, the years 2004 and 2005 will be shown as significant turning points in the student housing investment property niche. This real estate investment niche—once considered one of the lower-rung "get your hands dirty" and "let the kids party" fraternity house type investments—met Wall Street and institutional money in a big way in 2004 and 2005. The end of 2004 and early 2005 saw in succession the three first-ever initial public offerings of real estate companies devoted principally to ownership of student housing rental properties on major university campuses across the nation. By all accounts, based on the bid prices at which the stocks are trading and the large amount of dollars raised, Wall Street investors love the student housing niche.

Three well-capitalized real estate investment trusts (REITs) focused in this niche have raised equity in the public markets and are now actively traded on the New York Stock Exchange. In order of their public offerings, the companies and their stock trading symbols are American Campus Communities (ACC), GMH Communities Trust (GCT), and Education Realty Trust (EDR).

The importance of this recent development cannot be overstated for the student housing investment property niche. Of course, the REITs are well-funded and powerful competitors for real estate entrepreneurs in or entering the student housing investment niche. But consider this great news for the business. By raising the profile of the industry, student housing investments have gained the respect and interest of hungry mortgage lenders and high-net-worth individual joint venture and syndication partner investors. The pump has been primed. This means there's a hunger for well-researched and financially sound student housing investment opportunities. The large REITs won't get in the way of conducting deals in small, midsize, and even large range on many great college campuses. On the whole, I've found the increased respectability and investor focus on the student housing niche has made it easier to get deals completed.

It's important and useful to get to know the new Big Three of the student housing business. Besides, if you like to invest in stocks—as many of us real estate deal junkies do—and you believe in the long-term prospects of the student housing niche, you might consider buying student housing REITs stock, as I have. Not only have I made money on these stocks, I've learned a great deal about the continuing evolution of the student housing business from the public companies' annual reports, SEC filings, analysts' reports, and quarterly earnings forecast conference calls.

AMERICAN CAMPUS COMMUNITIES

The first company solely devoted to the student housing real estate investment niche to ever go public is American Campus Communities (ACC). It completed its initial public offering on August 12, 2004, selling more than 12 million shares for a total offering price of $220 million. Less than a year later, ACC completed a secondary stock offering, raising an additional $100 million or so in July of 2005. At the time of the secondary stock offering, the company owned or managed 43 student housing properties representing 26,900 beds. President and CEO of ACC William C. Bayless, Jr., is experienced and well respected within the student housing industry.

ACC owns and operates a growing portfolio of student housing properties. It's announced an aggressive acquisition strategy to continue to grow operations and use its $300+ million in equity raised through the sale of common stock to the public.

ACC business segments can be divided into three categories within the student housing niche:

1. Ownership and operation of company-owned student housing properties within close proximity to universities;
2. Development and construction management services for student housing properties owned by universities, charitable foundations, and others; and
3. Third-party management and leasing services for student housing properties owned by others.

The segment scheduled to produce the largest growth and focus is the ownership and operation of student housing properties as a result of the announced aggressive acquisitions program.

Although third-party management agreements, development, and construction service arrangements will be pursued, the majority of ACC's growth has come from adding student housing properties to the owned portfolio through acquisition and development. ACC is focusing on a cross between a dormitory and a traditional apartment. Its properties are usually located out of the core of the campus town, but within a few miles of the center of campus. Featuring garden-style apartment units, the typical ACC community is rich in amenities and includes on-site supervision.

A majority of the company's communities feature swimming pools, suntanning booths, recreational facilities, and even sand volleyball or basketball courts. Security is tighter at ACC properties than at other privately owned student housing properties, with most communities having residence advisors (RAs) living at the community, similar to a university-owned dormitory. Most of the company properties are leased on a by-the-bed basis, with parental guarantees, without joint-and-several liability of all of the roommates.

ACC has announced its acquisition strategy that only allows acquisitions on campuses with student housing shortages and low university-owned-beds-to-students ratios. At the time of the initial public offering, the company-owned student housing properties were located on campuses with university-owned-beds-to-students ratios averaging 18 percent. With only 18 percent of the total student housing needs being met on campuses of interest to ACC, the company went public in the fall of 2004 with an enviable 93.7 percent occupancy rate at its properties.

Although ACC has made several strategic acquisitions (mostly in high growth sun states) since its public offerings, its owned properties at the time of the initial offering included coverage at the following campuses:

Arizona State University
California State University at Fresno
California State University at San Bernardino
Temple University
Texas A&M University
University of Central Florida
University of Colorado at Boulder
University of Georgia–Athens
Virginia Polytechnic Institute

GMH COMMUNITIES TRUST

GMC Communities Trust (GCT) completed its initial public offering on October 28, 2004, with the issuance of more than 30 million shares of common stock for an aggregate initial public offering sales price in excess of $364 million.

Unlike the other Big Three student housing REITs, GMH Communities doesn't focus exclusively on the student housing niche. In addition to a large student housing portfolio, the company is also active in the military housing market, providing housing to the U.S. military and their families. Chairman, President, and Chief Executive Officer Gary M. Holloway, Sr., is a well-respected seasoned student housing industry professional.

The student housing division of GMH Communities operates more than 40,000 beds under the division name College Park Communities. The company continues to aggressively acquire student housing properties on major university campuses. GMC student housing communities are typically similar to the ACC property type, featuring large garden-style complexes adjacent to, but not in, the center of campus.

GMC College Park Communities apartment complexes feature high-end, resort-style accommodations of new construction with swimming pools, clubhouses, and sand volleyball courts. Bedrooms are usually fully furnished and have high-speed Internet access. Commonly, its by-the-bed leases include all utility charges. Communities are staffed with property and maintenance managers as well as assigned residence advisors. College Park Communities markets its properties as "student lifestyle" communities.

As of December 31, 2004, College Park Communities student housing properties had an average occupancy level of 94.2 percent, represented by a portfolio of 30 properties located near 25 colleges and universities in 19 states. It acquired eight additional student housing properties from January through March of 2005.

The company continues to make acquisitions aggressively and has a number of properties under contract and nonbinding letters of intent.

GMH student housing properties include a major presence at the following university campuses:

Ball State University
Bowling Green University
California State University–Sacramento
East Carolina University
Georgia Southern University
Louisiana State University
Michigan State University
Middle Tennessee State University
Minnesota State University–Mankato
North Texas University
Penn State University
Texas Tech University
University of Alabama–Birmingham
University of California–Riverside
University of Florida
University of Illinois–Urbana/Champaign
University of Michigan–Ann Arbor
University of Mississippi
University of Nebraska–Lincoln
University of Nevada–Reno
University of North Carolina–Chapel Hill
University of North Carolina–Charlotte
University of Northern Iowa
University of Oklahoma
University of South Carolina
University of Southern Mississippi
University of Tennessee
University of Virginia

University of Wyoming
Western Michigan University
West Virginia University

Similar to ACC, GMH manages student housing apartment communities owned by third parties for a fee, in addition to its own student housing portfolio. According to its policy, GMH prefers to acquire existing and completed student housing properties rather than engage in new construction development directly.

EDUCATION REALTY TRUST

With a completed initial public offering on January 31, 2005, Education Realty Trust (EDR) was the most recent of the Big Three to go public. The net proceeds of the initial offering, after expenses, were approximately $321 million.

The predecessor company of Education Realty Trust was Allen & O'Hara, a well-respected student housing industry firm with more than 40 years of experience as an owner and manager of student housing properties. Simultaneous with the initial public offering, the company purchased 14 student housing communities previously owned by the JPI Group, a large, previously private, student housing property owner. Headed by yet another well-respected and experienced chairman, chief executive officer, and president, Education Realty Trust is overseen by Paul O. Bower.

In addition to its ownership of student housing properties for its own account, like the other Big Three, EDR manages student housing properties for unrelated owners. The company also provides third-party consulting services for universities and others regarding student housing markets and facilities planning. Education Realty Trust properties usually feature a high level of amenities, have an average age of six years, and support a residence advisor program.

Education Realty Trust has also announced an aggressive acquisition strategy to deploy public offering equity money and grow the company. More than any other company I'm aware of, EDR stresses community building and student life. Its communities feature social activities, study skills counseling, and career development training, and sponsor parent and student appreciation events.

The company, like the other REITs, operates its facilities as a hybrid between a true private traditional apartment building and a dormitory. EDR is a by-the-bed rather than joint-and-several liability rental company (i.e., each student and the parental guarantor are only responsible for the lease payment of a single bedroom with no liability for the full rent due on the unit). Rent payments include common area amenities and utilities, and often Internet and cable TV charges. Although I'm not a fan of the by-the-bed lease, Education Realty Trust uses other landlord-favorable provisions in its standard lease to protect the property's income stream.

For example, under the standard company lease, students pay a nonrefundable service fee in addition to an application fee. The service fee is retained to pay for the cost of redecorating the unit at the end of the lease term. Rental units are inspected on a quarterly basis for damage and needed repairs. Any damages are repaired each quarter and charged to the student's account for immediate collection. Not only are apartments kept in good condition throughout the year, but the quarterly repair procedure reduces large, end-of-academic-year repairs and charges. In addition, provisions are contained in the standard EDR lease to hold student residents responsible for any damage caused anywhere on the property by their visitors.

EDR has been active in pursuing acquisitions since its initial public offering. In addition to the 14 properties purchased simultaneously with the offering from JPI Properties, a flurry of other acquisitions has taken place. As of August of 2005, Educational

Realty Trust owns or manages student housing properties near the following university campuses:

Alabama A&M University
Auburn University
Augusta State University
Bloomsburg University of Pennsylvania
California State University–San Marcos
Clarion University of Pennsylvania
Clemson University
Community College of Denver
Florida A&M University
Florida State University
Kalamazoo Valley Community College
Lock Haven University of Pennsylvania
Metropolitan State College of Denver
Middle Tennessee State University
North Carolina State University
Ohio State University
Oklahoma State University
Penn State
Purdue University–West Lafayette
Salisbury University
Tallahassee Community College
Texas Tech University
University of Arizona
University of Central Florida
University of Cincinnati
University of Colorado–Denver
University of Florida
University of Georgia
University of Illinois–Urbana/Champaign
University of Kansas
University of Louisville

University of Mississippi
University of Missouri
University of North Carolina
University of Northern Colorado
University of Oklahoma
University of South Carolina
University of South Florida
University of Tennessee
Western Kentucky University
Western Michigan University

Education Realty Trust seeks a diversity of student housing property types including garden-style, midrise, and highrise student housing apartment buildings. The firm also actively pursues the acquisition or management of private dormitory-style student housing. EDR is not afraid to be a pioneer in small, less-known college towns. It's represented in a large number of campus markets with a single student housing asset rather than a concentration of multiple student housing assets on a smaller number of campuses.

INSTITUTIONAL MONEY COMES TO CAMPUS

Along with the recent initial public offerings, the student housing investment market niche has seen the inflow of institutional money as well. Major stockholders in the Big Three REITs include institutional investors and large fund managers. In addition, institutional money is readily available to fund both the equity and debt portions of well-underwritten student housing investment property transactions.

Some investors might get scared out of the market as a result of not wanting to compete with the Big Three and institutional investors. I see these developments as a confirmation of the viability of the student housing niche. It makes me feel confident in my enthusiasm for the student housing niche as a great way to generate cash flow and build a substantial net worth for the future.

COME ON DOWN!

I'm sure you can tell by now that I love real estate investing and being a real estate entrepreneur. The real estate investment business is still wide open to anyone—of any income or wealth level—willing to acquire the knowledge necessary to handle transactions and build great wealth.

In my experience, real estate opportunities are always available in any market to astute investors who stay well versed. Fresh opportunities particularly attract entrepreneurs who can find specialty niches within the field.

Whether you are brand new to real estate investing or have a number of deals under your belt, you can't afford to ignore the student housing niche as a way to create current cash flow and long-term appreciation in net worth.

THIS STUDENT HOUSING NICHE IS FOR REAL

The demographic data compiled by the U.S. Census Bureau makes the case for the continued need for student housing near major university campuses. Here's the winning trend triad:

1. Increases in the size of the population turning 18 over the next decade as the echo boomer generation turns college age,
2. An increasing percentage of high school graduates enrolling in college, and
3. Increased budget pressures restricting university spending on new dormitory construction.

These assure a bright future for well-located student housing properties. A large influx of student housing renters will soon arrive at college campuses. This trend won't reverse. The die has been cast!

Proceed with Caution

However, smart investors will enter this market cautiously. Every student housing opportunity doesn't equal a great real estate investment. As with any real estate investment property, the numbers need to be crunched and the cash flow has to exist for a transaction to make sense. With student housing, the location of the state and university also has to make sense. Because many universities have plenty of competing dorm rooms and restrictive policies preventing students from living in private housing, proceed with caution.

By using the techniques and data contained in this book, you will have a guide to choosing the right state and university campus with the best chance for future appreciation and high occupancy. By carefully selecting college campuses in high growth states, with open student housing policies, on large public university campuses with high enrollment and an aging housing stock, you can tip the odds in your favor to create a successful wealth-building real estate investment. Although no real estate investment can be absolutely perfect and without some risk, by aligning factors important to the student housing niche in your favor, you are likely to be successful.

Remember that, nationally, the university provides only 20 percent of the housing needs of enrolled university students in school-owned beds. Most college students already rely on the private sector to provide their housing while away from home pursuing a college degree.

Given that 80 percent of the student college town population looks to rent a place to live from private real estate owners, I don't know about you, but I'd want to own property close to campus and be the landlord. I already went through college as a student (and those were some great years). I've gone back to college as a landlord and am enjoying it just as much—actually, even more!

GETTING THE DEAL DONE

Lacking personal funds is no longer a barrier to entry into the real estate investment business; it shouldn't keep you from entering the student housing niche. If you can learn the techniques described in this book to identify and locate quality student housing property investments and work hard at the business, you can put the funds together to carry out the transaction. Using the techniques described, you will raise the equity and arrange the financing to close on quality student housing transactions.

After you are in this business for a while, you'll see that finding the money to handle student housing real estate deals is the easy part. The hard part is finding a property worth buying.

Persistence is key. You'll find you'll learn to look at and walk away from most deals. But keep at it. Keep driving to campuses and taking property tours, run the pro forma income and expense numbers, conduct the rent surveys, and make the projections. Eventually, you'll find the property that makes sense to buy. And when it all comes together and you close on the transaction, you'll have accomplished a great deal. You'll have set in place a current cash flow generator and wealth builder for you and your family's future.

The student housing market niche provides many avenues for investors to get in on the action. Although buying a single condominium or a detached single-family home in a college town gets you into the market in a small way, I'm partial to buying apartment buildings. In fact, I'm so sold on the future of student housing that I'm putting investor groups together to buy as many good student housing apartment properties on the "right" campuses that I can find.

Active real estate developers may choose to enter this market with new construction projects and rehabs of older student housing properties. Sophisticated investors can enter by acquiring and operating privately owned university-approved dormitories. A smaller but growing niche within the student housing niche is new construction and condominium conversion projects near or adjacent to college campuses. A trend toward senior housing retirement communities adjacent to major campuses has even begun.

Identify Risks Up Front

Realize that all real estate investments carry various degrees of risk. Prudent investors identify risks up front and take action to limit the potential risks in an investment.

The student housing niche carries its own unique set of risks that must be identified and managed. By recognizing and controlling the risks outlined in this book, you can take the steps necessary to limit the downside and make prudent, profitable real estate investments. By going in with your eyes wide open, and facing potential problem issues, you can limit your risks and make investments with the greatest chance for success.

WALL STREET COMES TO CAMPUS

With the recent initial public offering and listing on the New York Stock Exchange of three large real estate investment trusts specializing in student housing, we now have a Big Three in student housing. However, the business is still wide open to private individual investors and partnership groups. Of all the college campuses I visit—and this business brings me to hundreds of them—I find multiple real estate entrepreneur success stories. Ownership of real estate in general and the student housing stock in particular remains widely fragmented; no one firm dominates the market.

The truth is, Wall Street and institutional money are trying to catch up to you and me (collectively, all individual and partnership group real estate investors) when it comes to owning student housing assets. The "big money boys" may have discovered the business as well—should we be flattered?—but the student housing niche still belongs to you and me!

YOU CAN DO THIS, TOO

By beginning with small deals and building a track record, you'll work up to large transactions and see a growing number of opportunities. If you start with a little wealth and want to grow it, use this head start to your advantage and get going now.

If you're an experienced real estate investor and feel comfortable handling large transactions, open your checkbook and dust off your lines of credit. Jump in—but with your eyes wide open. It still happens; you can invest in well-located multihousing properties on a college campus and realize an immediate occupancy level of 100 percent with almost no rent collection loss.

If you're willing to work hard and stay educated within the student housing market, you will make money and build your net worth. Invest smart and use the knowledge you've gained from this book to succeed in this student housing niche. Don't hold back. As a friend first told me, "You can do this!" He was right. And so can you.

APPENDIXES

The pages that follow provide investors interested in the student housing real estate niche with many tools. Use the sample letters and forms to help locate and acquire quality housing.

Be sure to use the Appendix materials as a general guide that you can adapt to the circumstances of your particular real estate transactions. They aren't meant to be exhaustive, but they will serve as excellent patterns.

A

STATE-BY-STATE GUIDE TO MARKETS OF OPPORTUNITY

The following state-by-state guide is meant as a beginning point for the serious student housing investor searching for markets of opportunity in which to make a student housing acquisition.

By starting with the raw data provided here, and applying the due diligence techniques described in the text of the book, you'll greatly increase your chances for a successful student housing real estate investment.

Alabama

Largest University in State:	Auburn University
Number of Students Enrolled Fall 2004:	22,928
University-Owned Beds Fall 2004:	3,400
School-Owned-Beds-to-Students Ratio:	14.82%
Beds-to-Students Favorability Rating for Investors:	Highly Favorable

Colleges and universities with enrollments exceeding 10,000 full-time undergraduate students enrolled in Fall 2003:

University of Alabama–Tuscaloosa   14,270 Enrolled

Alaska

Largest University in State:	U. of Alaska–Anchorage
Number of Students Enrolled Fall 2004:	17,512
University-Owned Beds Fall 2004:	950
School-Owned-Beds-to-Students Ratio:	5.42%
Beds-to-Students Favorability Rating for Investors:	Highly Favorable

Colleges and universities with enrollments exceeding 10,000 full-time undergraduate students enrolled in Fall 2003:

None

Arizona

Largest University in State:	Arizona State University
Number of Students Enrolled Fall 2004:	49,171
University-Owned Beds Fall 2004:	5,600
School-Owned-Beds-to-Students Ratio:	11.38%
Beds-to-Students Favorability Rating for Investors:	Highly Favorable

Colleges and universities with enrollments exceeding 10,000 full-time undergraduate students enrolled in Fall 2003:

Northern Arizona University–Flagstaff   11,034 Enrolled
University of Arizona–Tucson   24,217 Enrolled

Arkansas

Largest University in State:	University of Arkansas

Number of Students Enrolled Fall 2004:   16,461
University-Owned Beds Fall 2004:   3,200
School-Owned-Beds-to-Students Ratio: 19.43%
Beds-to-Students Favorability Rating for
    Investors: Highly Favorable
Colleges and universities with enrollments exceeding 10,000 full-time
*   undergraduate students enrolled in Fall 2003:*
None

California

Largest University in State: University of
                            California–L.A.
Number of Students Enrolled Fall 2004:   37,563
University-Owned Beds Fall 2004:   7,200
School-Owned-Beds-to-Students Ratio: 19.16%
Beds-to-Students Favorability Rating for
    Investors: Highly Favorable
Colleges and universities with enrollments exceeding 10,000 full-time
*   undergraduate students enrolled in Fall 2003:*

Cal State Polytechnic University–Pomona	14,611 Enrolled
California State University–Chico	12,580 Enrolled
California State University–Fresno	14,294 Enrolled
California State University–Fullerton	18,720 Enrolled
California State University–Long Beach	21,678 Enrolled
California State University–Los Angeles	10,435 Enrolled
California State University–Northridge	19,605 Enrolled
California State University–Sacramento	17,202 Enrolled
Cal Poly–San Luis Obispo	6,425 Enrolled
San Diego State University	21,697 Enrolled
San Francisco State University	16,407 Enrolled
San Jose State University	15,431 Enrolled
University of California–Berkeley	21,942 Enrolled
University of California–Davis	20,962 Enrolled

University of California–Irvine   19,201 Enrolled
University of California–Riverside   13,940 Enrolled
University of California–San Diego   19,602 Enrolled
University of California–Santa Barbara   17,199 Enrolled
University of California–Santa Cruz   13,002 Enrolled
University of Southern California–L.A.   15,687 Enrolled

Colorado

Largest University in State: U. of Colorado–
                                             Boulder
Number of Students Enrolled Fall 2004:   29,151
University-Owned Beds Fall 2004:   7,100
School-Owned-Beds-to-Students Ratio: 24.35%
Beds-to-Students Favorability Rating for
     Investors: Favorable
*Colleges and universities with enrollments exceeding 10,000 full-time
     undergraduate students enrolled in Fall 2003:*
Colorado State University–Fort Collins   19,078 Enrolled
Metropolitan State College of Denver   11,772 Enrolled

Connecticut

Largest University in State: University of
                                             Connecticut
Number of Students Enrolled Fall 2004:   23,179
University-Owned Beds Fall 2004:   11,000
School-Owned-Beds-to-Students Ratio: 47.45%
Beds-to-Students Favorability Rating for
     Investors: Highly Unfavorable
*Colleges and universities with enrollments exceeding 10,000 full-time
     undergraduate students enrolled in Fall 2003:*
None

Delaware

Largest University in State:	University of Delaware
Number of Students Enrolled Fall 2004:	19,418
University-Owned Beds Fall 2004:	7,000
School-Owned-Beds-to-Students Ratio:	36.04%
Beds-to-Students Favorability Rating for Investors:	Unfavorable

Colleges and universities with enrollments exceeding 10,000 full-time undergraduate students enrolled in Fall 2003:
None

Florida

Largest University in State:	University of Florida
Number of Students Enrolled Fall 2004:	47,000
University-Owned Beds Fall 2004:	7,600
School-Owned-Beds-to-Students Ratio:	16.17%
Beds-to-Students Favorability Rating for Investors:	Highly Favorable

Colleges and universities with enrollments exceeding 10,000 full-time undergraduate students enrolled in Fall 2003:

Florida Atlantic University–Boca Raton	10,699 Enrolled
Florida International University–Miami	16,355 Enrolled
Florida State University–Tallahassee	25,959 Enrolled
University of Central Florida–Orlando	25,757 Enrolled
University of South Florida–Tampa	21,604 Enrolled

Georgia

Largest University in State:	University of Georgia
Number of Students Enrolled Fall 2004:	30,824

University-Owned Beds Fall 2004:   5,800
School-Owned-Beds-to-Students Ratio: 18.81%
Beds-to-Students Favorability Rating for
    Investors: Favorable
Colleges and universities with enrollments exceeding 10,000 full-time
    undergraduate students enrolled in Fall 2003:
Georgia Institute of Technology–Atlanta   10,367 Enrolled
Georgia Southern University–Statesboro   12,247 Enrolled
Georgia State University–Atlanta   13,511 Enrolled
Kennesaw State University–Kennesaw   10,045 Enrolled

Hawaii

Largest University in State: University of
                                      Hawaii–Manoa
Number of Students Enrolled Fall 2004:   20,549
University-Owned Beds Fall 2004:   3,000
School-Owned-Beds-to-Students Ratio: 14.59%
Beds-to-Students Favorability Rating for
    Investors: Highly Favorable
Colleges and universities with enrollments exceeding 10,000 full-time
    undergraduate students enrolled in Fall 2003:
None

Idaho

Largest University in State: Boise State
                                        University
Number of Students Enrolled Fall 2004:   18,456
University-Owned Beds Fall 2004:   850
School-Owned-Beds-to-Students Ratio: 4.60%
Beds-to-Students Favorability Rating for
    Investors: Highly Favorable
Colleges and universities with enrollments exceeding 10,000 full-time
    undergraduate students enrolled in Fall 2003:
None

Illinois

Largest University in State:	University of Illinois–Urbana/ Champaign
Number of Students Enrolled Fall 2004:	38,291
University-Owned Beds Fall 2004:	10,855
School-Owned-Beds-to-Students Ratio:	28.34%
Beds-to-Students Favorability Rating for Investors:	Favorable

Colleges and universities with enrollments exceeding 10,000 full-time undergraduate students enrolled in Fall 2003:

DePaul University–Chicago	10,847 Enrolled
Illinois State University–Normal	16,811 Enrolled
Northern Illinois University–DeKalb	16,398 Enrolled
Southern Illinois University–Carbondale	14,675 Enrolled
University of Illinois–Chicago	14,276 Enrolled

Indiana

Largest University in State:	Indiana University– Bloomington
Number of Students Enrolled Fall 2004:	37,821
University-Owned Beds Fall 2004:	13,000
School-Owned-Beds-to-Students Ratio:	34.37%
Beds-to-Students Favorability Rating for Investors:	Neutral

Colleges and universities with enrollments exceeding 10,000 full-time undergraduate students enrolled in Fall 2003:

Ball State University	16,319 Enrolled
Indiana University/Purdue University– Indianapolis	13,371 Enrolled
Purdue University–West Lafayette	29,051 Enrolled

Iowa

Largest University in State:	University of Iowa
Number of Students Enrolled Fall 2004:	29,745
University-Owned Beds Fall 2004:	5,600
School-Owned-Beds-to-Students Ratio:	18.82%
Beds-to-Students Favorability Rating for Investors:	Favorable

Colleges and universities with enrollments exceeding 10,000 full-time undergraduate students enrolled in Fall 2003:

Iowa State University–Ames	20,682 Enrolled
University of Northern Iowa–Cedar Falls	10,484 Enrolled

Kansas

Largest University in State:	University of Kansas
Number of Students Enrolled Fall 2004:	28,849
University-Owned Beds Fall 2004:	5,500
School-Owned-Beds-to-Students Ratio:	19.06%
Beds-to-Students Favorability Rating for Investors:	Highly Favorable

Colleges and universities with enrollments exceeding 10,000 full-time undergraduate students enrolled in Fall 2003:

Kansas State University–Manhattan	16,285 Enrolled

Kentucky

Largest University in State:	University of Kentucky
Number of Students Enrolled Fall 2004:	26,545
University-Owned Beds Fall 2004:	5,100
School-Owned-Beds-to-Students Ratio:	19.21%
Beds-to-Students Favorability Rating for Investors:	Highly Favorable

Colleges and universities with enrollments exceeding 10,000 full-time undergraduate students enrolled in Fall 2003:

Eastern Kentucky University–Richmond   10,449 Enrolled
University of Louisville   10,676 Enrolled
Western Kentucky University–Bowling Green 12,931 Enrolled

Louisiana

Largest University in State: Louisiana State
                                                 University
Number of Students Enrolled Fall 2004:   30,000
University-Owned Beds Fall 2004:   7,600
School-Owned-Beds-to-Students Ratio: 25.33%
Beds-to-Students Favorability Rating for
    Investors: Favorable

Colleges and universities with enrollments exceeding 10,000 full-time undergraduate students enrolled in Fall 2003:

University of Louisiana–Lafayette   12,025 Enrolled

Maine

Largest University in State: University of
                                                 Southern Maine
Number of Students Enrolled Fall 2004:   11,007
University-Owned Beds Fall 2004:   1,600
School-Owned-Beds-to-Students Ratio: 14.53%
Beds-to-Students Favorability Rating for
    Investors: Highly Favorable

Colleges and universities with enrollments exceeding 10,000 full-time undergraduate students enrolled in Fall 2003:

None

Maryland

Largest University in State:	University of Maryland– College Park
Number of Students Enrolled Fall 2004:	34,933
University-Owned Beds Fall 2004:	8,700
School-Owned-Beds-to-Students Ratio:	12.36%
Beds-to-Students Favorability Rating for Investors:	Highly Favorable

Colleges and universities with enrollments exceeding 10,000 full-time undergraduate students enrolled in Fall 2003:

Towson University–Towson	12,051 Enrolled

Massachusetts

Largest University in State:	Boston University
Number of Students Enrolled Fall 2004:	26,704
University-Owned Beds Fall 2004:	11,000
School-Owned-Beds-to-Students Ratio:	41.19%
Beds-to-Students Favorability Rating for Investors:	Highly Unfavorable

Colleges and universities with enrollments exceeding 10,000 full-time undergraduate students enrolled in Fall 2003:

Northeastern University–Boston	14,492 Enrolled
University of Massachusetts–Amherst	17,379 Enrolled

Michigan

Largest University in State:	Michigan State University
Number of Students Enrolled Fall 2004:	44,836
University-Owned Beds Fall 2004:	17,000
School-Owned-Beds-to-Students Ratio:	37.91%
Beds-to-Students Favorability Rating for Investors:	Unfavorable

Colleges and universities with enrollments exceeding 10,000 full-time undergraduate students enrolled in Fall 2003:

Central Michigan University–Mount Pleasant	17,090 Enrolled
Eastern Michigan University–Ypsilanti	13,573 Enrolled
Grand Valley State University–Allendale	15,002 Enrolled
University of Michigan–Ann Arbor	23,312 Enrolled
Wayne State University–Detroit	11,004 Enrolled
Western Michigan University–Kalamazoo	20,248 Enrolled

Minnesota

Largest University in State:	University of Minnesota–Twin Cities
Number of Students Enrolled Fall 2004:	50,954
University-Owned Beds Fall 2004:	6,300
School-Owned-Beds-to-Students Ratio:	12.36%
Beds-to-Students Favorability Rating for Investors:	Highly Favorable

Colleges and universities with enrollments exceeding 10,000 full-time undergraduate students enrolled in Fall 2003:

Minnesota State University–Mankato	11,189 Enrolled
St. Cloud State University–St. Cloud	11,790 Enrolled

Mississippi

Largest University in State:	Mississippi State University
Number of Students Enrolled Fall 2004:	15,416
University-Owned Beds Fall 2004:	4,000
School-Owned-Beds-to-Students Ratio:	25.94%
Beds-to-Students Favorability Rating for Investors:	Favorable

Colleges and universities with enrollments exceeding 10,000 full-time undergraduate students enrolled in Fall 2003:

University of Mississippi–Oxford	10,079 Enrolled

Missouri

Largest University in State:	University of Missouri–Columbia
Number of Students Enrolled Fall 2004:	25,527
University-Owned Beds Fall 2004:	10,000
School-Owned-Beds-to-Students Ratio:	39.17%
Beds-to-Students Favorability Rating for Investors:	Unfavorable

Colleges and universities with enrollments exceeding 10,000 full-time undergraduate students enrolled in Fall 2003:

Southwest Missouri State University–Springfield	12,449 Enrolled

Montana

Largest University in State:	University of Montana–Missoula
Number of Students Enrolled Fall 2004:	13,352
University-Owned Beds Fall 2004:	4,500
School-Owned-Beds-to-Students Ratio:	33.70%
Beds-to-Students Favorability Rating for Investors:	Neutral

Colleges and universities with enrollments exceeding 10,000 full-time undergraduate students enrolled in Fall 2003:

None

Nebraska

Largest University in State:	University of Nebraska–Lincoln
Number of Students Enrolled Fall 2004:	21,792

University-Owned Beds Fall 2004:   5,600
School-Owned-Beds-to-Students Ratio: 25.69%
Beds-to-Students Favorability Rating for
    Investors: Favorable
Colleges and universities with enrollments exceeding 10,000 full-time
    undergraduate students enrolled in Fall 2003:
None

Nevada

Largest University in State: University of
    Nevada–Las
    Vegas
Number of Students Enrolled Fall 2004:   27,000
University-Owned Beds Fall 2004:   1,500
School-Owned-Beds-to-Students Ratio: 5.5%
Beds-to-Students Favorability Rating for
    Investors: Highly Favorable
Colleges and universities with enrollments exceeding 10,000 full-time
    undergraduate students enrolled in Fall 2003:
None

New Hampshire

Largest University in State: University of New
    Hampshire
Number of Students Enrolled Fall 2004:   12,000
University-Owned Beds Fall 2004:   5,500
School-Owned-Beds-to-Students Ratio: 45.83%
Beds-to-Students Favorability Rating for
    Investors: Highly Unfavorable
Colleges and universities with enrollments exceeding 10,000 full-time
    undergraduate students enrolled in Fall 2003:
None

New Jersey

Largest University in State:	Rutgers State University–New Brunswick
Number of Students Enrolled Fall 2004:	34,694
University-Owned Beds Fall 2004:	14,000
School-Owned-Beds-to-Students Ratio:	40.34%
Beds-to-Students Favorability Rating for Investors:	Highly Unfavorable

Colleges and universities with enrollments exceeding 10,000 full-time undergraduate students enrolled in Fall 2003:

None

New Mexico

Largest University in State:	University of New Mexico
Number of Students Enrolled Fall 2004:	25,031
University-Owned Beds Fall 2004:	2,400
School-Owned-Beds-to-Students Ratio:	9.58%
Beds-to-Students Favorability Rating for Investors:	Highly Favorable

Colleges and universities with enrollments exceeding 10,000 full-time undergraduate students enrolled in Fall 2003:

New Mexico State University–Las Cruces   10,538 Enrolled

New York

Largest University in State:	New York University
Number of Students Enrolled Fall 2004:	38,188
University-Owned Beds Fall 2004:	11,000
School-Owned-Beds-to-Students Ratio:	28.80%
Beds-to-Students Favorability Rating for Investors:	Favorable

Colleges and universities with enrollments exceeding 10,000 full-time undergraduate students enrolled in Fall 2003:

Cornell University–Ithaca	13,655 Enrolled
CUNY–Hunter College–New York	10,489 Enrolled
Rochester Institute of Technology	10,652 Enrolled
St. John's University–Jamaica	11,841 Enrolled
SUNY–Albany	10,692 Enrolled
SUNY–Binghamton	10,292 Enrolled
SUNY–Stony Brook	12,710 Enrolled
Syracuse University–Syracuse	11,455 Enrolled
University of Buffalo–SUNY	16,219 Enrolled

North Carolina

Largest University in State:	North Carolina State University
Number of Students Enrolled Fall 2004:	29,637
University-Owned Beds Fall 2004:	6,700
School-Owned-Beds-to-Students Ratio:	22.60%
Beds-to-Students Favorability Rating for Investors:	Favorable

Colleges and universities with enrollments exceeding 10,000 full-time undergraduate students enrolled in Fall 2003:

Appalachian State University–Boone	11,833 Enrolled
East Carolina University–Greenville	15,348 Enrolled
University of North Carolina–Chapel Hill	15,355 Enrolled
University of North Carolina–Charlotte	12,191 Enrolled

North Dakota

Largest University in State:	University of North Dakota
Number of Students Enrolled Fall 2004:	13,187
University-Owned Beds Fall 2004:	3,200
School-Owned-Beds-to-Students Ratio:	24.26%

Beds-to-Students Favorability Rating for
    Investors: Favorable
Colleges and universities with enrollments exceeding 10,000 full-time
    undergraduate students enrolled in Fall 2003:
None

Ohio

Largest University in State:	Ohio State University
Number of Students Enrolled Fall 2004:	50,995
University-Owned Beds Fall 2004:	9,200
School-Owned-Beds-to-Students Ratio:	18.04%
Beds-to-Students Favorability Rating for Investors:	Highly Favorable

Colleges and universities with enrollments exceeding 10,000 full-time
    undergraduate students enrolled in Fall 2003:

Bowling Green State University–Bowling Green	14,462 Enrolled
Kent State University–Kent	15,982 Enrolled
Miami University–Oxford	14,769 Enrolled
Ohio University–Athens	16,053 Enrolled
University of Akron	13,926 Enrolled
University of Cincinnati	15,725 Enrolled
University of Toledo	13,773 Enrolled
Wright State University–Dayton	10,000 Enrolled

Oklahoma

Largest University in State:	University of Oklahoma
Number of Students Enrolled Fall 2004:	24,569
University-Owned Beds Fall 2004:	4,300
School-Owned-Beds-to-Students Ratio:	17.50%
Beds-to-Students Favorability Rating for Investors:	Highly Favorable

Colleges and universities with enrollments exceeding 10,000 full-time
undergraduate students enrolled in Fall 2003:

Oklahoma State University–Stillwater   16,402 Enrolled

Oregon

Largest University in State:	Portland State University
Number of Students Enrolled Fall 2004:	21,348
University-Owned Beds Fall 2004:	1,600
School-Owned-Beds-to-Students Ratio:	7.49%
Beds-to-Students Favorability Rating for Investors:	Highly Favorable

Colleges and universities with enrollments exceeding 10,000 full-time
undergraduate students enrolled in Fall 2003:

Oregon State University–Corvallis	13,987 Enrolled
University of Oregon–Eugene	14,452 Enrolled

Pennsylvania

Largest University in State:	Pennsylvania State University
Number of Students Enrolled Fall 2004:	41,289
University-Owned Beds Fall 2004:	12,000
School-Owned-Beds-to-Students Ratio:	29.06%
Beds-to-Students Favorability Rating for Investors:	Favorable

Colleges and universities with enrollments exceeding 10,000 full-time
undergraduate students enrolled in Fall 2003:

Indiana University of Pennsylvania–Indiana	11,191 Enrolled
Temple University–Philadelphia	18,917 Enrolled
University of Pittsburgh–Pittsburgh	15,141 Enrolled

Rhode Island

Largest University in State:	University of Rhode Island
Number of Students Enrolled Fall 2004:	13,435
University-Owned Beds Fall 2004:	3,900
School-Owned-Beds-to-Students Ratio:	29.02%
Beds-to-Students Favorability Rating for Investors:	Favorable

Colleges and universities with enrollments exceeding 10,000 full-time undergraduate students enrolled in Fall 2003:
None

South Carolina

Largest University in State:	University of South Carolina–Columbia
Number of Students Enrolled Fall 2004:	25,596
University-Owned Beds Fall 2004:	6,800
School-Owned-Beds-to-Students Ratio:	26.56%
Beds-to-Students Favorability Rating for Investors:	Favorable

Colleges and universities with enrollments exceeding 10,000 full-time undergraduate students enrolled in Fall 2003:
Clemson University–Clemson   12,857 Enrolled

South Dakota

Largest University in State:	South Dakota State University
Number of Students Enrolled Fall 2004:	10,954
University-Owned Beds Fall 2004:	3,400
School-Owned-Beds-to-Students Ratio:	31.03%
Beds-to-Students Favorability Rating for Investors:	Neutral

Colleges and universities with enrollments exceeding 10,000 full-time undergraduate students enrolled in Fall 2003:
None

Tennessee

Largest University in State:	University of Tennessee– Knoxville
Number of Students Enrolled Fall 2004:	27,800
University-Owned Beds Fall 2004:	7,300
School-Owned-Beds-to-Students Ratio:	26.25%
Beds-to-Students Favorability Rating for Investors:	Favorable

Colleges and universities with enrollments exceeding 10,000 full-time undergraduate students enrolled in Fall 2003:

Middle Tennessee State University– Murfreesboro	16,626 Enrolled
University of Memphis	11,256 Enrolled

Texas

Largest University in State:	University of Texas–Austin
Number of Students Enrolled Fall 2004:	50,000
University-Owned Beds Fall 2004:	6,600
School-Owned-Beds-to-Students Ratio:	13.12%
Beds-to-Students Favorability Rating for Investors:	Highly Favorable

Colleges and universities with enrollments exceeding 10,000 full-time undergraduate students enrolled in Fall 2003:

Baylor University–Waco	11,260 Enrolled
Texas A&M University–College Station	32,818 Enrolled
Texas State University–San Marcos	17,679 Enrolled
Texas Tech University–Lubbock	21,030 Enrolled

University of Houston	19,112 Enrolled
University of North Texas–Denton	18,654 Enrolled
University of Texas–Arlington	13,486 Enrolled
University of Texas–El Paso	10,990 Enrolled
University of Texas–San Antonio	15,584 Enrolled

Utah

Largest University in State:	Brigham Young University
Number of Students Enrolled Fall 2004:	29,932
University-Owned Beds Fall 2004:	6,500
School-Owned-Beds-to-Students Ratio:	21.17%
Beds-to-Students Favorability Rating for Investors:	Favorable

Colleges and universities with enrollments exceeding 10,000 full-time undergraduate students enrolled in Fall 2003:

University of Utah–Salt Lake City	15,242 Enrolled
Utah State University–Logan	11,772 Enrolled
Utah Valley State College–Orem	12,477 Enrolled
Weber State University–Ogden	11,015 Enrolled

Vermont

Largest University in State:	University of Vermont
Number of Students Enrolled Fall 2004:	9,273
University-Owned Beds Fall 2004:	4,000
School-Owned-Beds-to-Students Ratio:	43.13%
Beds-to-Students Favorability Rating for Investors:	Highly Unfavorable

Colleges and universities with enrollments exceeding 10,000 full-time undergraduate students enrolled in Fall 2003:

None

Virginia

Largest University in State: Virginia Tech–
                                                     Blacksburg
Number of Students Enrolled Fall 2004:   25,420
University-Owned Beds Fall 2004:   8,900
School-Owned-Beds-to-Students Ratio: 35.01%
Beds-to-Students Favorability Rating for
    Investors: Neutral
*Colleges and universities with enrollments exceeding 10,000 full-time
    undergraduate students enrolled in Fall 2003:*
George Mason University–Fairfax   12,796 Enrolled
James Madison University–Harrisonburg   14,354 Enrolled
University of Virginia–Charlottesville   13,050 Enrolled
Virginia Commonwealth University   13,998 Enrolled

Washington

Largest University in State: University of
                                                     Washington
Number of Students Enrolled Fall 2004:   39,199
University-Owned Beds Fall 2004:   5,000
School-Owned-Beds-to-Students Ratio: 12.75%
Beds-to-Students Favorability Rating for
    Investors: Highly Favorable
*Colleges and universities with enrollments exceeding 10,000 full-time
    undergraduate students enrolled in Fall 2003:*
Washington State University–Pullman   15,826 Enrolled
Western Washington University–Bellingham   11,451 Enrolled

West Virginia

Largest University in State: West Virginia
                                                     University
Number of Students Enrolled Fall 2004:   25,255

University-Owned Beds Fall 2004:   3,600
School-Owned-Beds-to-Students Ratio: 14.25%
Beds-to-Students Favorability Rating for
    Investors: Highly Favorable
Colleges and universities with enrollments exceeding 10,000 full-time
    undergraduate students enrolled in Fall 2003:
None

Wisconsin

Largest University In State: University of
                                        Wisconsin–
                                        Madison
Number of Students Enrolled Fall 2004:   41,588
University-Owned Beds Fall 2004:   11,000
School-Owned-Beds-to-Students Ratio: 26.44%
Beds-to-Students Favorability Rating for
    Investors: Favorable
Colleges and universities with enrollments exceeding 10,000 full-time
    undergraduate students enrolled in Fall 2003:
University of Wisconsin–Milwaukee   16,816 Enrolled

Wyoming

Largest University in State: University of
                                          Wyoming
Number of Students Enrolled Fall 2004:   12,012
University-Owned Beds Fall 2004:   2,800
School-Owned-Beds-to-Students Ratio: 23.32%
Beds-to-Students Favorability Rating for
    Investors: Favorable
Colleges and universities with enrollments exceeding 10,000 full-time
    undergraduate students enrolled in Fall 2003:
None

B

SAMPLE LETTER OF INTENT FOR STUDENT HOUSING TRANSACTION

Following is a sample Letter of Intent our firm uses in connection with making initial offers to purchase student housing properties. It's meant as a guide and should be adapted to meet the needs and issues of a particular real estate transaction. *Note: I strongly suggest that you have an attorney review any letter you copy or adapt before sending it out.*

SAMPLE LETTER OF INTENT

Via e-mail xxxxxx@msm.com and Federal Express Next Day Delivery

XXXXXXXX XXXXXXXXX
XXXXXXXXXX Realtors
1234 Any Street
Any Town, USA 99999

Re: Insert Property Address Here

Dear XXXXX:

This letter of intent will evidence the intent of a to-be-formed LLC affiliated with our company or its assignee or designee (the "Purchaser") to enter into a contract of purchase with the Owner of Record (the "Seller") for the purchase by Purchaser of the real estate property commonly known as "Insert Property Address Here" with a total of "Insert Number of Units Here" apartment units (the "Property"). The purchase by Buyer shall be on the terms and subject to the conditions set forth below:

1. At the closing of the transaction (the Closing), Seller shall sell the property to Purchaser free and clear of all liens, encumbrances, claims, or interests of any kind other than existing leases and other exceptions permitted as set forth in the legally binding, written agreement to be negotiated and entered into by Purchaser and Seller.

2. **Purchase Price:** In consideration of the sale and transfer of the property, Purchaser shall pay the Seller the total sum of Four Million Dollars ($4,000,000), adjusted for prorations, at closing, for rent and other similar items ("Purchase Price").

3. **Earnest Money:** The purchase price shall be payable with an earnest money deposit, to be held by "Insert Name of Listing Broker here" Realtors, to bear interest for the benefit of Purchaser of the sum of $100,000 due upon execution of this letter of intent and the $3,900,000 balance, plus or minus prorations, payable to Seller at closing.

4. **Commission:** Seller agrees to pay all real estate sales commission due "List names of any brokers here" in connection with the transaction. Seller and Purchaser warrant there are no other brokers entitled to compensation in connection with the transaction.

5. **Due Diligence Period:** The obligation of Purchaser to purchase the property is conditioned upon the performance by Purchaser of such inspections and due diligence as Purchaser deems appropriate or necessary including, but not limited to, appraisal, financial and lender due diligence, environmental, structural, and mechanical inspections of the land and improvements mak-

ing up the Property. Purchaser shall complete all such inspections and due diligence on or before "Insert End of Due Diligence Date Here." Seller shall fully cooperate with Purchaser in connection with such inspections and due diligence and allow Purchaser, and Purchaser's representatives, access, upon reasonable notice, to the property, and will provide Purchaser with any information Purchaser deems reasonably necessary or desirable in connection with such inspections and due diligence. If at any time prior to "Insert End of Due Diligence Date Here," Purchaser determines in Purchaser's sole judgment that the property is unacceptable to Purchaser, for any reason or no reason, written notice shall be given to Seller, or Seller's agent, stating that the property has been rejected and thereupon, this letter of intent and subsequent contract for the purchase of the property shall be deemed null and void and all monies deposited as earnest money by Buyer shall immediately be returned to Buyer.

6. Seller shall allow Purchaser, and Purchaser's representatives, access to the property, upon reasonable notice, at reasonable times, prior to the closing of the transaction.

7. Seller shall install a new shingle roof on the property prior to and as a condition to the closing of this transaction. In addition, Seller shall be responsible for all apartment unit makeready and turnover costs and shall make all apartments ready for occupancy in connection with the August, 2005, turnover and fall semester term occupancy. Seller shall return the 2004/2005 lease security deposits to tenants who have terminated their leases pursuant to the terms of the leases.

8. The purchase contemplated herein includes substantial personal property including, but not limited to, partially furnished apartment units, appliances, kitchens, and other personal property. Seller shall furnish a schedule of all personal property to be included in the purchase within ten days of acceptance of this Letter of Intent.

9. Seller will assign all leases per the attached rent roll beginning August, 2005. As of the date of this Letter of Intent, all units,

with the exception of units 4 and 6 (two vacant units) at the property have in place leases for the 2005/2006 school year. The vacant units 4 and 6 shall be rented for the 12-month school year at $880 per month rent each prior to closing. If at the closing the vacant units have not been rented for the school year, Seller will pay Buyer the sum of $10,560 for each vacant unit.

10. Purchaser and Seller agree to use their best efforts to (a) enter a legally binding contract of purchase within five days, and (b) close the transaction contemplated hereby on "Insert Closing Date Here."

11. The Purchaser and Seller agree that this Letter of Intent outlines the terms and conditions upon which Purchaser will enter a legally binding agreement to purchase the Property from Seller and that the purchase of the Property is specifically conditioned upon the completion of the inspections required under number 5 above, to the satisfaction of the Purchaser. The final legally binding agreement to purchase and all sale documents must be in a form acceptable to both Purchaser and Seller and their respective legal counsel.

Very truly yours,

Michael H. Zaransky, CEO

This Letter of Intent is void and withdrawn if not accepted with an executed copy returned to Purchaser on or before "Insert Deadline for Acceptance Date Here."

Acknowledged and agreed to:
Seller:

_____

Date

Required Disclosure: Michael H. Zaransky, Barbara J. Gaffen, some of their affiliates, and Prime Property Investors, Ltd., are licensed Real Estate Brokers in the State of Illinois.

C

SAMPLE RIDER TO
REAL ESTATE CONTRACT

Following is our company's form for a Rider to a real estate contract for a typical student housing transaction. Because every transaction is unique, the form will require modifications. *Note: I strongly suggest that you have an attorney review any rider you copy or adapt before sending it out.*

While the Rider form and our typical offers complement a contract that is an all-cash offer (without mortgage contingencies), the Rider makes provisions for a due diligence review period. The Rider prevents the Seller from executing leases without consent prior to closing, allowing you access to the property prior to closing, further specification of the personal property made a part of the sale, a Seller's minimum rent guarantee, and the potential for a management agreement at a set fee with an entity related to the Seller.

SAMPLE RIDER TO REAL ESTATE SALES CONTRACT

This Rider is attached to and made a part of that certain contract dated December 15, 2004, for the purchase of the real estate commonly known as XXXXXX, College Town, USA.

1. **Due Diligence Period:** The obligation of Purchaser to purchase the property is conditioned upon the performance by Purchaser of such inspections and due diligence as Purchaser deems appropriate or necessary including, but not limited to, appraisal, financial due diligence, and environmental, structural, and mechanical inspections of the land and improvements comprising the Property. Purchaser shall complete all such inspections and due diligence on or before February 28, 2005. Seller shall fully cooperate with Purchaser in connection with such inspections and due diligence and allow Purchaser, and Purchaser's representatives, access, upon reasonable notice, to the property, and will provide Purchaser with any information Purchaser deems reasonably necessary or desirable in connection with such inspections and due diligence. If at any time prior to February 28, 2005, Buyer determines in Buyer's sole judgment that the property is unacceptable to Buyer, for any reason or no reason, written notice shall be given to Seller, or Seller's agent, stating that the property has been rejected and thereupon, this contract shall be deemed null and void and all monies deposited as earnest money by Buyer shall immediately be returned to Buyer.

2. Upon acceptance of this contract, Seller shall not enter any new leases or extensions of existing leases, other than on a month-to-month basis, for any rental space at the property without the advance written consent of the Purchaser.

3. Seller shall allow Purchaser access to the property, upon reasonable notice, at reasonable times, prior to the closing of the transaction.

4. The purchase contemplated herein includes substantial personal property including, but not limited to, fully furnished town

house properties, appliances, kitchens, and other personal property. Seller shall furnish a schedule of all personal property to be included in the purchase within ten days of acceptance of the contract.

5. Sellers will guarantee Buyer a "minimum gross income stream" on in-place leases at closing, covering the 2005/2006 school year, effective for the 12-month period beginning May 1, 2005, to April 30, 2006, of $575,000. "Minimum gross income stream" shall be determined at closing by taking the aggregate of all payments due on in-place leases covering the property for the specified period. Should the aggregate of all payments due for the specified lease period calculate to an amount lower than the $575,000 minimum guarantee, Seller shall pay the difference to Buyer at closing.

6. At Buyer's option, Seller shall cause _____ to enter into a management agreement (Manager-Owner Agreement) covering the property, upon terms and conditions acceptable to _____ and Buyer with a management fee equal to 8 percent of gross monthly rental income.

Required Disclosure: Barbara J. Gaffen and Michael H. Zaransky, principals of Purchaser and Prime Property Investors, Ltd., are licensed Real Estate Brokers in the State of Illinois.

December 15, 2004

Purchaser: Seller:

_____   _____

Prime Property Acquisitions, LLC,
As nominee for an Illinois Limited
Liability Company to be formed,
Michael H. Zaransky, Member

DUE DILIGENCE CHECKLIST FOR STUDENT HOUSING TRANSACTION

Following is the due diligence checklist developed by our firm in connection with the acquisition of student housing properties. The list is by no means all-inclusive of every item many investors examine during a due diligence period in connection with a real estate transaction. Particular issues and circumstances of a specific transaction may dictate expansion or contraction of the items to be covered on the due diligence checklist.

UNIVERSITY STUDENT HOUSING DUE DILIGENCE REVIEW CHECKLIST

Data Furnished by Sellers Independently Verified or Tested

1. Full accountants' reports of income and expense for past three years plus current year to date
2. Copies of all leases for the new academic term

3. Copies of last year Real Estate and Personal Property Tax Bills
4. Copies of all utility and scavenger bills for last three years and current
5. Copies of paid repair and maintenance bills for last three years and current
6. Rental Payment Delinquency Reports
7. Current and next academic year Rent Roll
8. Schedule of Security Deposits
9. Schedule of Advance Rent Payments (last month's rent and other)
10. Copy of all invoices and contracts for major building improvements, including recent new roof
11. Copy of all environmental, engineering, and appraisal reports
12. List of names and phone numbers of all vendors
13. Copies of any property plans, blueprints, and room layouts for buildings
14. Copy of any existing management agreement and any written service contracts or warranties still in effect
15. Plat of survey
16. Copies of any correspondence or filings relating to any resident disputes, controversies, or litigation

Data and Inspection Performed or Verified by Third Parties or Buyer

1. Complete inspection of all apartments and common areas
2. Mechanical Systems Inspection
3. Roof and Structure Inspection
4. City Code compliance and Certificate of Occupancy
5. Inspection of Property Grounds and Parking Lot

6. Compilation of data on lease-up dates and rental rates for new academic term leases

Market-Specific Due Diligence

1. Verify enrollment data
2. Verify number of university-owned beds
3. Research University Master Plan and interview Housing Office Officials regarding any future plans for new dorm construction or existing dorm demolition
4. Collect data on quality of school and potential to attract continued increased pool of applicants
5. Collect demographic data on size of the echo boom generation turning college age over the next ten years in property state and neighboring states
6. Market student apartment rent survey for comparable student housing properties
7. Survey near-in and further-out student housing communities for amenity and occupancy comparisons
8. Review local City or Village Master Plan
9. Interview potential local third-party management companies
   - Opinion of Student Housing Market at subject property city
   - Opinion of Subject Property
   - Opinion as to ability to increase rents
   - Budget for operation of property
   - Quote for management of property

Order-Written Third-Party Reports

1. Phase I Environmental
2. Engineering

3. Roof Consultant
4. Appraisal
5. Survey
6. Title

E

REQUEST FOR FINANCING STUDENT HOUSING ACQUISITION

Following is a sample of a cover memo our firm uses to request financing for a student housing multi-family property acquisition. Be sure to adapt the actual content of the cover memo to your particular transaction.

Generally speaking, it has been my experience that by furnishing the items listed in the cover memo, the commercial mortgage broker will have enough information to obtain loan proposal quotes from potential lending sources.

SAMPLE REQUEST MEMO FOR FINANCING

To: Commercial Mortgage Brokerage Firm of Choice
From: Michael H. Zaransky
Re: ABC University Student Housing Acquisition 39 Units
152 Beds

As per our telephone conversation, we are under contract to purchase a 100 percent fully leased student housing apartment complex well located just two blocks from the center of the ABC campus. The property has in-place leases for all of the units covering the 2005/2006 academic year and has been fully occupied for the past several years.

ABC University, in College Town, USA, is an excellent student housing market. The Big Ten school has an enrollment of 38,653 students. There are only 11,523 university-owned beds in dormitories, requiring more than 70 percent of the students to rely on private landlords for their housing needs. Because of the tight housing market, ABC is the only Big Ten school to allow freshmen to live outside of the dorms.

I have attached the financial information, and other data, regarding the property. I have included the first-year Pro-Forma Income and Expense statements based on the in-place leases and the operating history of the property.

I have also sent historical financial statements and other documents that I can't e-mail via overnight delivery for Monday. The Pro-Forma applies a 3 percent vacancy factor despite the full occupancy and no delinquency loss history of the property. The Pro-Forma was prepared in connection with a review by a local campus management firm operating 450 student housing units at ABC, and retained by us as the third-party managers for the property. The management firm has indicated the potential for further savings through its master insurance program, higher-than-typical water and sewer charges that should be reversed by fixing leaky toilets and faucets, and other potential revenue enhancements. We have not factored these additional net income enhancements into our Pro-Forma. As you can see, our Pro-Forma results in a first-year NOI of $298,690.

Because of the housing shortage and the undermarket rents at the subject property, we feel there are significant opportunities for increases in NOI as early as Year 2. Although the property is in excellent shape with little deferred maintenance, we plan to fund an additional $50,000 in upfront cash capital improvements for cosmetic upgrades at the property in order to push rents to market. We have completed environmental and engineering due diligence and have clean reports.

The total purchase price is $4,000,000. We are seeking 80 percent financing for a five-year or ten-year term and are seeking interest-only payments for the first two or three years. Our closing date is September 30, 2005.

It appears that this is an ideal loan for a life insurance company or a conduit. After you have had an opportunity to review the attachments and the package delivered on Monday, please give me a call with an indication as to rates and availability for our loan request.

SAMPLE PRIVATE PLACEMENT MEMORANDUM

When our firm raises equity by taking in outside equity partners in syndication, we issue a Private Placement Memorandum furnished to potential investors. This narrative description of an actual student housing acquisition where we raised investor equity is taken from a section of the Private Placement Memorandum. You're welcome to use it as a guide for the collection of the data we have found necessary in order to raise money from outside investors. *Note: I strongly suggest that you have an attorney review any placement memorandum you copy or adapt before sending it out.*

You can adapt this to create a similar narrative for raising funds from an institutional investor, familiarize a potential joint venture partner with a transaction, or provide descriptive information to a lender.

ABC UNIVERSITY STUDENT HOUSING VENTURE

Student Housing Multifamily Apartment Property Niche

The need for privately owned near-campus student housing will be greatly enhanced because of three major factors: (1) The echo boom generation is reaching college age, boosting the number of people turning 18 over the next decade to 75 million, (2) an increasing percentage of high school graduates are enrolling in colleges and universities, and (3) public universities are under increased financial pressure caused by state budget deficits that limit funds available to pay for the cost of additional university-owned student housing.

According to a recent study by the National Multi Housing Council, "Student Housing 101: Where are the Opportunities?", as a result of the demographic trend increasing the number of college-age students, "student housing is becoming one of the apartment industry's most important niche opportunities." Because of the large increase in the population size of college-age students and the increased percentage of the population obtaining a post–high school education, university enrollments have been rapidly increasing.

Of 118 colleges and universities recently surveyed by *College Planning and Management Magazine,* the on-campus school-owned student housing capacity was, on average, only 23.7 percent of the total current student population. The remaining and projected increasing number of students must look for near-campus housing elsewhere. As colleges and universities remain unable to meet the demand for housing themselves, well-located privately owned student housing apartment buildings will continue to achieve high occupancy levels and increased cash flow. Occupancy levels and the ratio of rental income to operating expenses are often far superior in the student housing niche as compared to that of traditional apartment buildings.

Positive Demographic Trends

The current decade is ushering in a steady and significant increase in the number of school-age children and young adults. Primary schools through colleges will accommodate an estimated 94 million students by the end of the century, representing an increase of more than 42 million from 2000. By comparison, the school-age population rose by 30 million during the 20th century. As a result, demographic trends will be favorable towards demand for university education and accompanying student housing in the coming years. (See Figure F.1.)

The Echo Boom Generation Comes of Age

What makes this growth trend different from the surge in the late 1960s is that this most recent upswing is a long, rising wave, with no immediate falloff in sight. Bolstered by the baby boom echo and the millennial boom, college enrollment will stay on a strong course and continue to increase for several years. The U.S.

FIGURE F.1 *18- to 24-Year-Old Population, 2000–2010 (in thousands)*

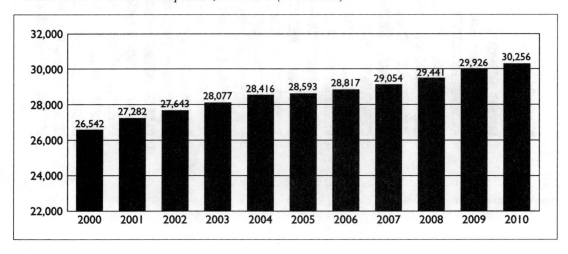

Department of Education projects that nationwide, enrollments will climb to 18.2 million students by 2013 for an increase of 1.8 million during the next decade alone. (See Figure F.2.)

ABC University–College Town, USA

The main campus of ABC University is located in College Town, USA, southwest of Chicago. The population of College Town is more than 140,000.

In 2003–2004, approximately $406 million was spent system-wide at ABC in support of research. The College Town campus

FIGURE F.2 *College Enrollment, 1988–2013 (in thousands)*

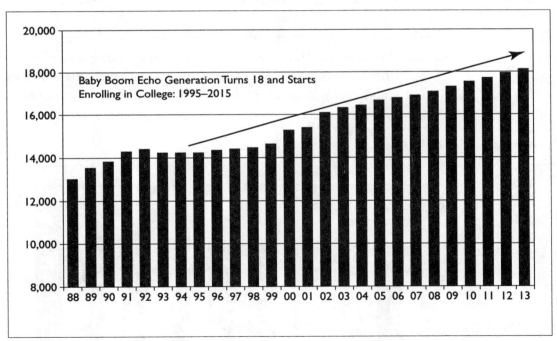

Source: Department of Education.

has 157 principal buildings on 2,307 acres. University lands provide space for ABC's two golf courses and the University Airport.

The focal point for future growth on the College Town campus at ABC is the 40-acre Discovery Park research facilities. Discovery Park also has been a key factor in ABC's success in raising more than $1 billion to date in the university's Campaign for ABC. Discovery Park is ABC's interdisciplinary research hub that brings the university's scientists, researchers, engineers, and management experts together on a project basis to discover ways to advance the Indiana economy and solve societal problems by inventing new products and processes. Also under construction at Discovery Park is a biomedical engineering building.

ABC University, in College Town, is an excellent student housing market. The Big Ten school had a Fall 2004 enrollment of 38,653 students. There are only 11,523 university-owned beds in dormitories, resulting in a university-owned-beds-to-enrolled-students ratio of 29.81 percent.

This student housing investor favorable ratio requires more than 70 percent of the ABC student body to rely on private landlords for their housing needs. Because of the tight housing market, ABC is the only Big Ten school to allow freshmen to live outside of the dorms.

Property Description

The subject property acquisition consists of two adjacent well-located student housing multifamily apartment properties. The buildings are located within easy walking distance of the center of campus and are within three blocks of the Memorial Student Union building. The properties feature a combined 39 apartment units with 152 beds. All apartments include a fully equipped kitchen with a stove, refrigerator, dishwasher, and microwave. The properties have a strong operating history and there are in-place leases equating to 100 percent occupancy for the Fall, 2005 academic school year. All leases provide for tenant-paid utilities, last month's rent, and security deposit up-front payments, and are joint-and-several-tenant liability contracts.

The 123 Main Street building is 3.5 stories and features 32 units, consisting of 30 4-Bedroom/2-Full Bath models and 2 3-Bedroom models for a total of 126 beds. The property was constructed in 1989, has 24 balconies and individual HVAC units and central air-conditioning in each apartment. The units are approximately 1,000 square feet in size and the property has 73 paved parking spaces.

The 456 Main Street building is a two-story building constructed in 1991. The property contains 6 4-Bedroom/2-Full Bath units, containing approximately 1,150 square feet, and 1 2-Bedroom/1-Full bath unit containing 650 square feet for a total of 26 beds. The building contains an additional 650-square-foot unit currently used as a management office. The property has 25 paved parking spaces.

Acquisition and Financing

The subject properties are being purchased for $4,000,000. Additional capital needs for closing costs and fees, aesthetic upgrades, initial capital improvements and reserves, and working capital are projected to be approximately $300,000. Therefore, the total capitalization of the transaction is projected to be $4,300,000. The Manager has executed a loan application with ABC Mortgage Capital ("ABC") for a loan to finance the acquisition of the Property. Terms include a loan in the amount of $3,200,000, a 10-year term with a fixed interest rate equal to 114 basis points over the 10-year Treasury security but not less than 5.20 percent. Based upon the 10-year Treasury as of the date of this memorandum, the fixed interest rate would be 5.20 percent.

The first 18 months will be interest only. Thereafter, the loan shall amortize based upon a 30-year schedule. The total equity to be raised to complete the transaction is $1,100,000. The transaction is projected to close by September 30, 2005.

The Manager, or affiliates and principals of its related companies, will invest, at a minimum, $400,000 of the total equity to be raised to complete the transaction.

Cash-Flow Projection Summary

Rents in place at the time of closing, under written lease agreements, will average $1,057 per unit per month. Rents due under in-place leases equal $41,222 per month, or $494,664 for 12 months. Rents are projected to increase by $60 per month per unit, or $15 per month per bed, during the second year of operations. Cash flow after debt service for the first three years of ownership is projected to be $124,000, $135,000, and $157,000, resulting in cash on cash returns of 9.53 percent, 10.33 percent, and 12.09 percent, respectively. Assuming a ten-year holding period, investors are projected to achieve a 14.00 percent IRR.

Asset Management Plan

The Manager believes that the investment will provide a current stable cash flow with upside potential. The Manager further believes that the investment is currently underperforming as in-place rents are under market for well-located student housing properties on the ABC campus. At closing, the Manager will establish a $50,000 reserve for projected capital improvements, including aesthetic and cosmetic upgrades.

The Manager has contracted with a well-established third-party ABC campus–based student housing apartment Management Company to manage the property and market the units for the Fall 2006 academic term. With property upgrades, professional management, and an aggressive lease-up marketing campaign, the Manager anticipates an early lease-up, at increased rents, for the Fall 2006 school year, effective in August of 2006.

The Manager believes there are additional cash-flow enhancement opportunities not reflected in the Manager's projections for the property. Additional cash-flow enhancement opportunities to be pursued by the Manager as a part of the Asset Management Plan include placement of entity-owned washers and dryers in the laundry rooms at the property upon expiration of the unfavorable laundry room lease agreements in 2007, providing wireless Internet connections for residents for a modest monthly fee, charging a fee for parking as near-campus parking availability continues to tighten, converting the current on-site management office into a revenue-producing apartment, close monitoring of operating expenses, and taking measures through preventative maintenance to lower the above-average water and sewer expenses at the property.

For conservative underwriting purposes, it is important to note that none of the potential revenue and cash-flow enhancement methods have been factored into the investment projections. Additionally, a capital expense reserve is being prefunded and, during each year of operations, an additional amount is being allocated to the capital reserve account. In the absence of any revenue enhancements or second-year rent increase to market, based upon in-place leases, the Property is projected to yield in excess of 9.5 percent in Year 1.

Michael H. Zaransky graduated from the University of Illinois at Champaign-Urbana as a James Scholar. He's also a graduate of Northwestern University School of Law.

A licensed real estate broker in the State of Illinois since 1979, he is a founder and co-CEO of Prime Property Investors, Ltd., based in Northbrook, Illinois. His firm has received industry recognition and numerous awards for its real estate projects. It has been named one of the 50 best companies in residential construction and development to work for by *Professional Builder* magazine.

Zaransky has published numerous articles on the subject of real estate investment, including the student housing niche. A past featured monthly columnist in *The Chicago Realtor,* he founded the first citywide Commercial and Investment Real Estate Awards Dinner in Chicago.

A speaker at many professional real estate investment groups, he has moderated numerous panel discussions and has been quoted in local and national publications. Recognized in his community as a leader in the real estate investment field, Zaransky is active in a large number of trade organizations and has built an extensive network of professional contacts. He currently serves on the board of directors and executive committee of the Chicago Association of Realtors and is past chairman of the association's commercial and investment division.

Zaransky's professional affiliations include:

- National Apartment Association
- Chicago Association of Realtors
- National Association of Realtors

- Urban Land Institute
- National Multi Housing Council
- National Association of Home Builders
- University of Illinois Alumni Association
- Northwestern University Alumni Association
- Young Presidents Organization Alumni

Share the message!

Bulk discounts
Discounts start at only 10 copies and range from 30% to 55% off retail price based on quantity.

Custom publishing
Private label a cover with your organization's name and logo. Or, tailor information to your needs with a custom pamphlet that highlights specific chapters.

Ancillaries
Workshop outlines, videos, and other products are available on select titles.

Dynamic speakers
Engaging authors are available to share their expertise and insight at your event.

**Call Kaplan Publishing Corporate Sales at
1-800-621-9621, ext. 4444,
or e-mail kaplanpubsales@kaplan.com**